The Robert Burns Songbook
for Guitar and Voice

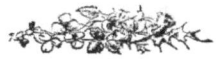

The Robert Burns Songbook for Guitar and Voice

Also Suitable for Guitar Duo or Flute/Recorder and Guitar

By Adrian Allan

Edited by Allan H. Jones

Cover design by Phil Ogden

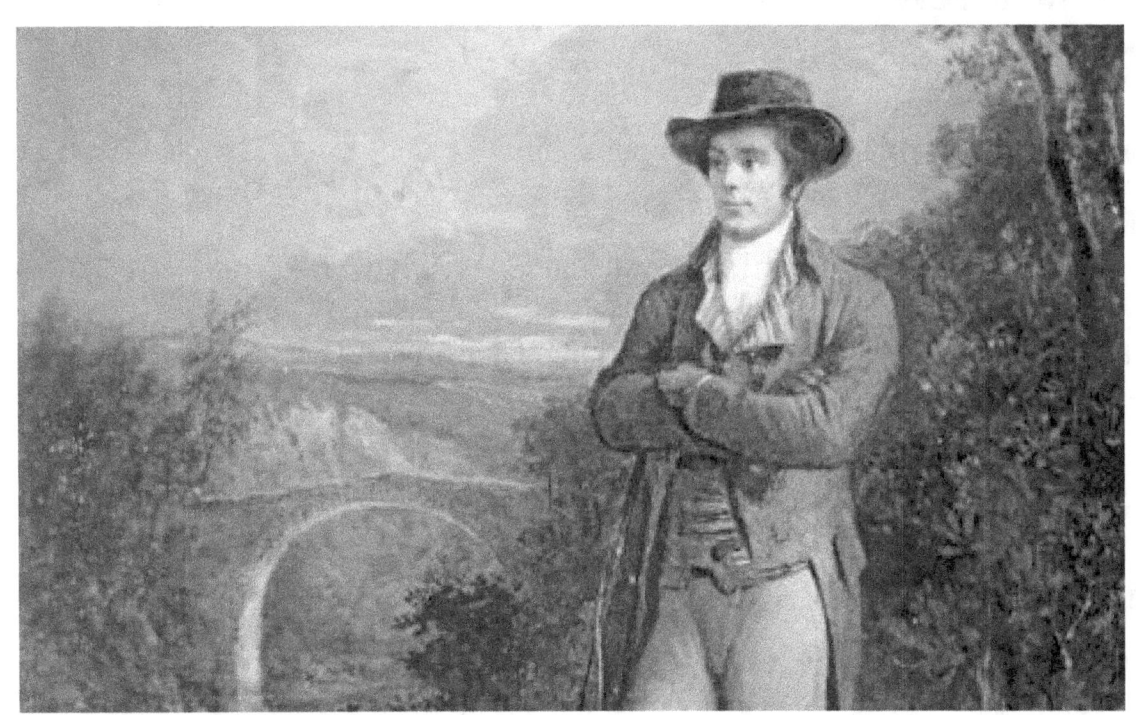

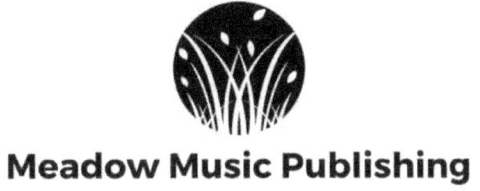

Meadow Music Publishing

First Printing: 2016

ISBN 978 - 1-326 - 63344 - 8

Meadow Music Publishing
23c Burford Road
Manchester, M16 8EW

Tel: 0161 881 2997

www.juliealford@btinternet.com.

www.facebook.com/meadowmusicpublishing/

Front cover illustration:
A detail from the Burns portrait by Alexander Nasmyth, 1828.

Other illustrations from The Illustrated Family Burns, 1870.

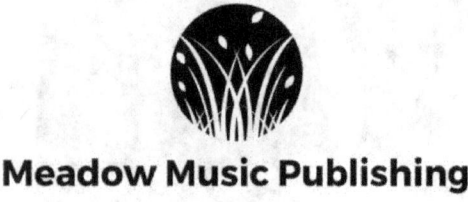

Meadow Music Publishing

Adrian Allan Website:

Meadow Music Publishing:

Dedication

This book is dedicated to Burns' fans the world over

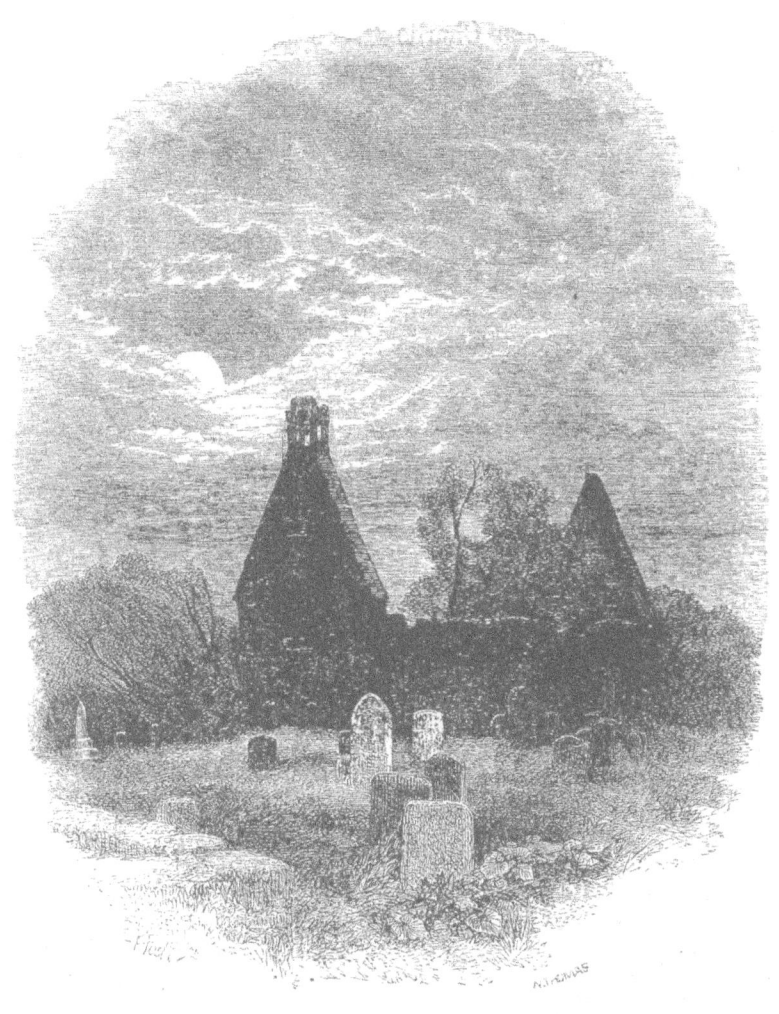

**Alloway Kirk, the setting of Burns' epic poem,
Tam o' Shanter**

Contents

Songs

Appendix 1 : Music Arranged For Guitar and Guitar/Flute/Recorder

Preface

Despite Robert Burns' pre-eminence in the culture and history of Scotland, the number of modern editions of his musical work is surprisingly limited. In compiling this guitar-vocal score, I have had to rely on a reprinted piano edition from the early part of the Twentieth Century, checking its accuracy with *The Scots Musical Museum* - the original six-volume work of Scottish song, to which Burns was the primary contributor.

There are no modern guitar editions of Burns' music, save for the ubiquitous "folk" books of lyrics plus guitar chord symbols; something that hardly constitutes a proper arrangement. However, it is clear that the music of Burns is uniquely suited to the subtleties and grace of the guitar as an accompanying instrument. In his time, the preferred folk instruments were the violin and the cittern, an instrument similar to the guitar.

I have chosen some of Burns' best-loved songs and set them to guitar accompaniments that are designed to be both idiomatic and effective accompaniments for the solo vocalist. Guitar-friendly keys have been used, and in some cases used scordatura (sixth and fifth strings re-tuned) has been utilised to add extra resonance and tone-colour. Chord diagrams are available for those who prefer the strumming approach. For reasons of clarity and simplicity, the chords do not always match some of the more complicated harmonic progressions in the notated guitar part. Ukulele chord diagrams are provided in the appendix.

I hope that this book will renew interest in some of the most beautiful songs in Scotland's musical heritage, and will bring the work of Burns to a Twenty-First Century audience.

How to Use This Book

I had always intended this book to be primarily for guitar players and singers, but I also wanted a resource for guitar and flute/recorder or other instruments in C. However, the range of some pieces is too low for flute or recorder, where the notes fall below Middle C. In such cases, I have provided alternative arrangements, specifically designed to better accommodate the range of recorder/flute, which can be found in the appendix. More advanced flute players may prefer to play some of the melodies an octave above the written pitch. In some cases, for example, in *Corn Rigs* and *Comin' Thro' the Rye*, there was no need to provide an alternative version; the written range will suit voice, guitar, flute or recorder.

In the vocal section of the book, the range should be comfortable for most singers, lying between A3 and E5. Male singers will sing the pieces down an octave.

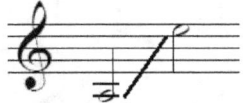

It is interesting to note that in the original arrangements submitted by Burns to *The Musical Museum*, the tessitura is quite high, with the G above the E not being uncommon (a note that many amateur singers will struggle to execute).

The reason for this may be that in the eighteenth century, concert pitch was not established and most probably, most keyboard instruments were pitched at least a semitone below A=440, which is the modern standard.

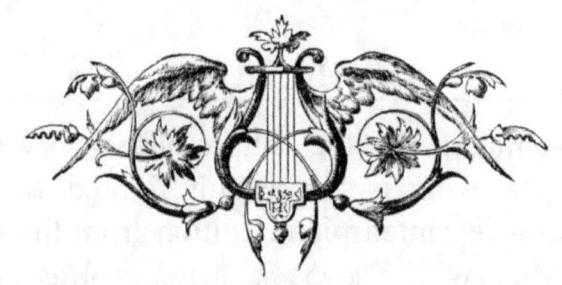

The Life of Robert Burns: A Brief Summary

- Robert Burns was born in 1759 in Ayr, on the west coast of Scotland to a self-educated tenant farmer, William Burnes, who would prove to be instrumental in Robert's education.

- In 1774, Robert Burns first started to write poetry; producing *O Once I Loved A Bonnie Lass*.

- In 1784, Burns first met his future wife, Jean Armour, who he married in 1788. She bore him nine children, but only three of them survived past infancy.

- Shortly afterwards, Burns fell in love with Mary Campbell (1763-1786), who inspired some of his songs and poems. Mary died of typhus in 1786.

- At around the same time Burns considered a job in Jamaica as a bookkeeper on a slave plantation.

- In 1786, A collection of Burns' poems was published; *Poems, Chiefly in the Scottish Dialect* (which became known as the *Kilmarnock Volume*) and gained him national fame. Burns travelled to Edinburgh and met Walter Scott and had his portrait (the cover of this book) painted by Alexander Nasmyth.

- In 1787 Burns contributed to *The Scots Musical Museum*, a collection of Scottish folk songs edited by James Johnson. Burns collected and modified hundreds of traditional songs, and the series ran to six volumes. Many of his best known songs originate from this series.

- Burns started to work as Excise Officer in Dumfries in 1789, abandoning farming as a source of income.

- Burns died in 1796 following a dental extraction. He had been suffering from rheumatic fever.

- Burns is reported to have over 600 living descendants in 2012.

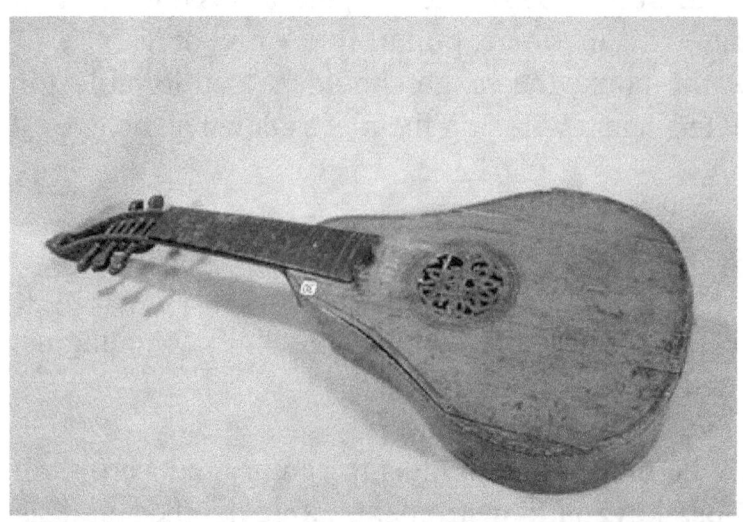

Burns' cittern in the Birthplace Museum, Alloway

Dear Brother

It will be no very pleasing news to you to be told that I am dangerously ill, & not likely to get better. — An inveterate rheumatism has reduced me to such a state of debility, & my appetite is totaly gone, so that I can scarce stand on my legs. — I have been a week at sea-bathing, & I will continue there or in a friend's house in the country all the summer — God help my wife & children, if I am taken from their head! — They will be poor indeed. — I have contracted one or two serious debts, partly from my illness these many months, & partly from too much thoughtlessness as to expense when I came to town that will cut in too much on the little I leave them in your hands. —

Remember me to my Mother. — yours

July 10th 1796.

R BURNS.

A letter from Robert Burns to his brother, Gilbert dated July 10 1796. He died on the 21st July.

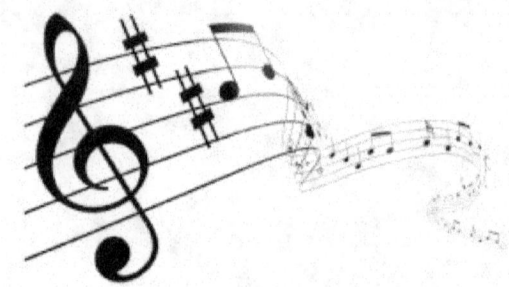

Robert Burns, Songwriting and Music

To what extent did Burns write his songs from scratch, or are they re-workings of older songs – and if so, are the melodies re-worked, or the words, or both?

This is the main question that is faced by scholars of Burns' songs, and one that is worth thinking about in the context of this present volume.

We know that Burns played the fiddle and could read music. It is also possible that he played the cittern, a guitar-like fretted instrument. Burns was highly educated and was aware of the works of contemporary European composers such as Mozart and Haydn.

However, nearly all of the songs attributed to Burns are not entirely the product of his own imagination, but are the end result of his craft in collecting and building upon existing songs; he had a seemingly innate ability to match words to music. In a 1778 letter to James Johnson, the editor of *The Musical Museum*, Burns states:

> I am in hopes that I shall pick some fine tunes from among the Collection of Highland airs which I got from you

It is known that Burns had in his possession collections of Scottish and Gaelic airs from which to match to words. Sometimes he would even use the melodies of contemporary fiddle players such as Niel Gow (1727-1807) as a basis for a song.

On other occasions, as is thought to be the case with the original *Auld Lang Syne*, the melody probably already existed in an almost compete form.

The lyrics of a Burns song were sometimes almost a literal reproduction of an already-existing song, but at the other extreme, could flow entirely from the pen of Burns himself.

However, it is thought that most of his songs lay somewhere in-between; Burns would borrow a line or a phrase from an existing song and craft it into a coherent whole.

It is worth bearing in mind that any Burns song inevitably raises a whole host of issues concerning provenance and authenticity. It is very hard to decide how much of the song was written by Burns, and how much was borrowed from a traditional source, either from a print or the oral/ "folk" tradition

The situation is further complicated further when we realise that many of the melodies that we associate with some of his most famous songs, such as *Ae Fond Kiss*, are quite different from what Burns originally intended.

Some Victorian tunesmiths re-worked Burns' songs and in a few instances, such as in the case of *Afton Water*, the newer melody has become as popular as the original.

We will never know if he would have approved of quasi-operatic renditions of his songs at Burns Suppers, or even the re-arrangement of his music for guitar and voice (however it is worth noting that *The Musical Museum* favoured a format of melody and figured bass, a sort of early form of chord symbols for keyboard players).

Perhaps these questions are best left for the scholars and researchers of Burns. As performers, we should let the music speak for itself.

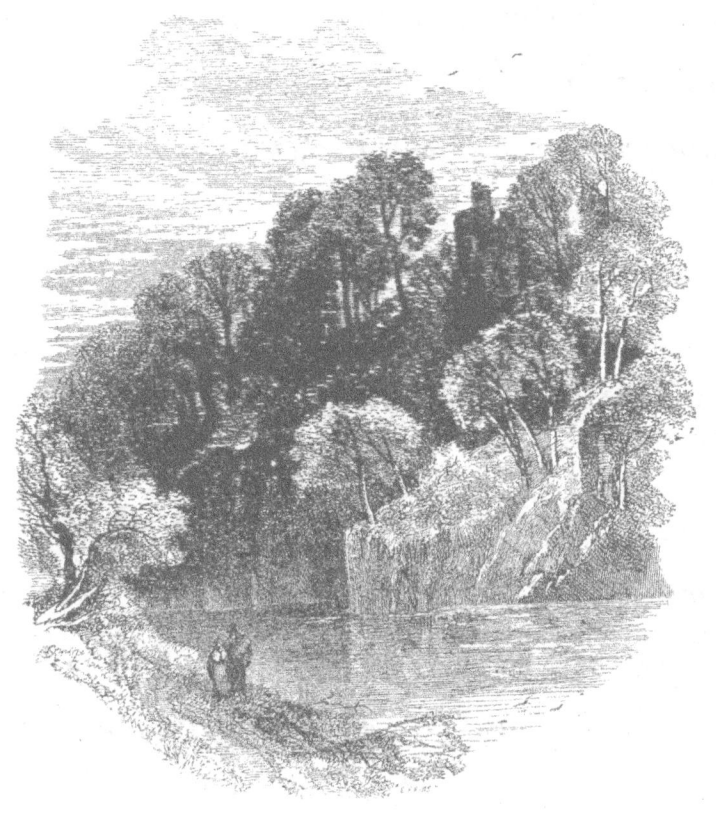

The banks of the Doon

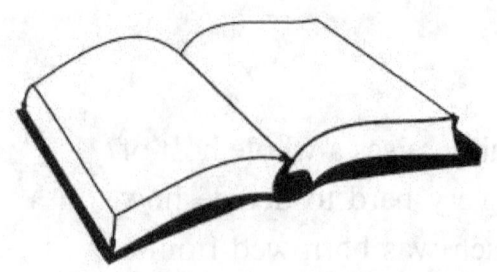

Robert Burns – His Education and Early Years

It is interesting to ask the question: how could the son of a struggling Eighteenth Century farmer have reached world-wide recognition for his literary and musical skills?

Aside from Burns' innate creative talents, the answer to that question can be traced in his formative years, where, despite the struggles of rural life, Burns received a first-rate education. Burns' father, William, was the early catalyst in Robert's learning. William taught Robert reading, writing, arithmetic, geography and history. In 1777 the family moved to a farm at Lochlea, near Tarbolton, and Burns describes the depth of his education at this time:

What I knew of ancient story was gathered from Salmon's and Guthrie's geographical grammars ; and the ideas I had formed of modern manners, of literature, and criticism, I got from the Spectator. These, with Pope's Works, some plays of Shakespeare, Tull and Dickson on Agriculture...... The collection of songs was my vade mecum. I pored over them driving my cart, or walking to labour, song by song, verse by verse: carefully noting the true, tender, or sublime, from affectation and fustian. I am convinced I owe to this practice much of my critic craft, such as it is.

William Burnes (the spelling of the family name before Robert) also employed eighteen-year-old John Murdoch as a teacher for his sons, Robert and Gilbert. Murdoch built upon the fine body of knowledge imparted by William. According to Gilbert:

With Murdoch we learned to read English tolerably well, and to write a little. He taught us, too, the English Grammar. I was too young to profit much by his lessons in grammar, but Robert made some proficiency in it, a circumstance of considerable weight in the unfolding of his genius and character; as he soon became remarkable for the fluency and correctness of his expression.

What is surprising is that Murdoch noted:

I attempted to teach them a little church-music. Here they were left far behind by all the rest of the school. Robert's ear, in particular, was remarkably dull, and his voice untunable. It was long before I could get them to distinguish one tune from another.

This did not seem an auspicious start for Scotland's most famous songwriter! Although William did not have a particular aptitude for mathematics, he made sure that his son did not miss out any branch of learning. In 1775, Robert was sent to Kirkoswald in south Ayrshire to study with Hugh Rodger. It was there that he learned "mensuration, surveying and dialling", as well as geometry and trigonometry. These skills would later prove useful for Robert in his employment in Excise Officer in the last period of his life.

Aside from formal education, and a voracious appetite for reading, we know that Robert Burns absorbed folk tales from both his mother and Betty Davidson, a widow of cousin of Burns' mother. According to Robert:

In my infant and boyish days too, I owed much to an old Maid of my Mother's, remarkable for her ignorance, credulity and superstition. She had, I suppose, the largest collection in the country of tales and songs concerning devils, ghosts, fairies, brownies, witches, warlocks, spunkies, kelpies, elf-candles, dead-lights, wraiths, apparitions, cantraips, giants, inchanted towers, dragons and other trumpetry

It is easy to see how this rich folklore fed into the creative imagination of young Robert, who would later pen his most famous work that is absolutely steeped in the supernatural, Tam O' Shanter. There were minor gaps in Burns' schooling; he never learned Latin, for example, a subject that was *de rigueur* amongst the learned elite. However, by any standards, Robert received an education that was by all accounts quite remarkable, given his social circumstances.

Robert Burns and Edinburgh

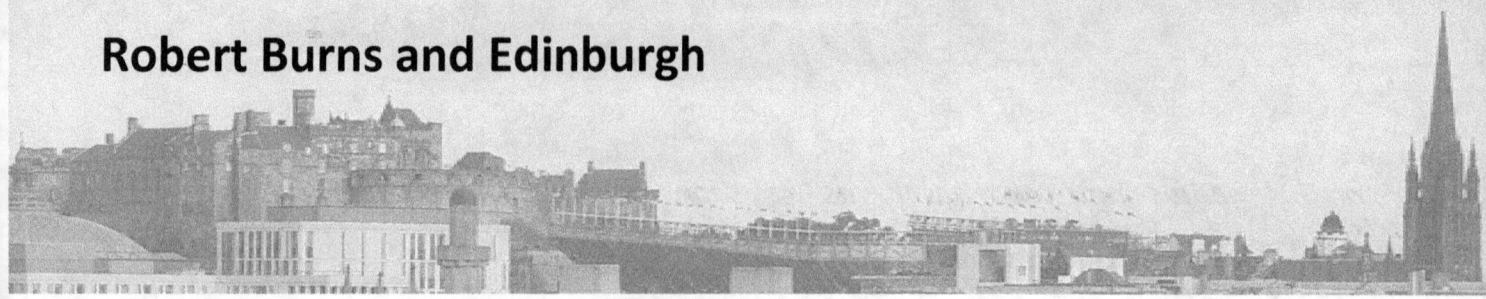

On 27 November 1786, Burns borrowed a pony and set out to Edinburgh. It was perhaps the most important decision of his career.

After the publication of *Poems, Chiefly in the Scottish Dialect*, members of the city's social elite were keen to make the acquaintance of the rustic poet from Ayrshire. The second edition of the work, the *Edinburgh Edition*, was dedicated to *The Noblemen and Gentlemen of the Caledonian Hunt* and 2,800 copies were despatched to 1,500 subscribers. The new edition included a specially commissioned portrait of Burns by Alexander Nasmyth.

Burns recognised the significance of and grandeur of the city of Edinburgh and was moved to write:

> *With awe-struck thought, and pitying tears,*
> *I view that noble, stately Dome,*
> *Where Scotia's kings of other years,*
> *Fam'd heroes! had their royal home...*
>
> *...Edina! Scotia's darling seat!*
> *All hail thy palaces and tow'rs;*
> *Where once, beneath a Monarch's feet,*
> *Sat Legislation's sovereign pow'rs:*
> *From marking wildly-scatt'red flow'rs,*
> *As on the banks of Ayr I stray'd,*
> *And singing, lone, the ling'ring hours,*
> *I shelter in thy honour'd shade.*

Robert Burns, Address to Edinburgh, 1786

It was in Edinburgh that Burns met a very young Walter Scott. Reminiscing back to the age of sixteen, Scott later wrote of Burns:

I think his countenance was more massive than it looks in any of the portraits ... there was a strong expression of shrewdness in all his lineaments; the eye alone, I think, indicated the poetical character and temperament. It was large, and of a dark cast, and literally glowed when he spoke with feeling or interest. I never saw such another eye in a human head, though I have seen the most distinguished men of my time.

One of the most productive friendships made in Edinburgh was made with the publisher James Johnson. Both Johnson and Burns shared an interest in Scottish song, and Burns agreed to make submissions to Johnson's six-volume *The Scots Musical Museum*. In all, Burns was responsible for around 200 songs in the whole collection, and the project was to occupy a large part of his later years, before his untimely death at the age of thirty seven.

Not all of Burns' associations with the city were quite so professional. When he first arrived, Burns took up residence in the Old Town, which was a maze of cobbled streets and run-down dwellings.

Burns was a regular at the *Crochallan Fencibles* drinking club, based at the Anchor Tavern on one of the streets that runs off the Royal Mile. Burns was introduced to the club by his publisher, William Smellie. By all accounts, it was a place where men drank, often to excess, and amused themselves by singing bawdy songs.

Agnes Maclehose, known to her friends as Nancy, was a competent young poet who lived in Edinburgh. She was determined to meet Burns, and did so in December 1787. After the meeting, the pair exchanged a series of love letters. They met in 1791 for the last time and it is believed that Burns wrote the song *Ae Fond Kiss* with Agnes in mind. She outlived Burns by 45 years and in 1831, wrote in her journal:

This day I can never forget. Parted with Burns, in the year 1791, never more to meet in this world. Oh, may we meet in Heaven.

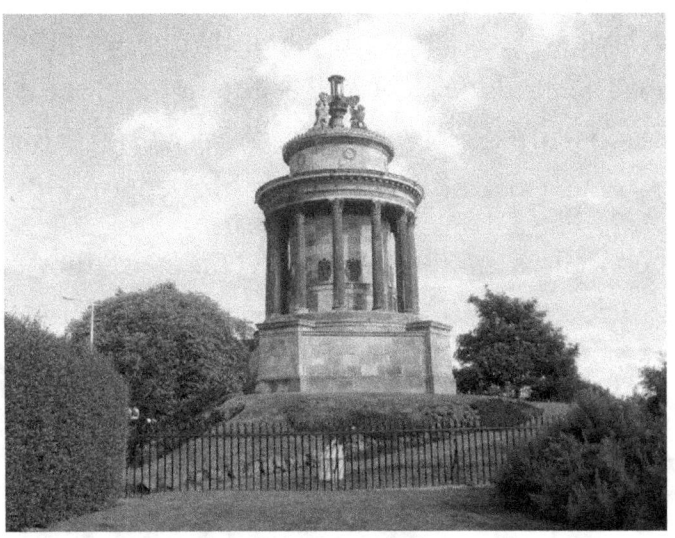

Burns monument, Calton Hill, Edinburgh

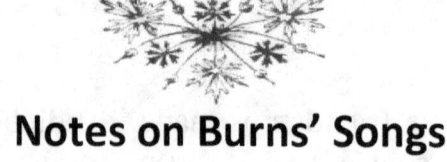

Notes on Burns' Songs

My Love is Like a Red, Red Rose. This song was originally paired with a tune known as *Major Graham* by Neil Gow. It was not until 1821 that it was matched with its now-familiar melody, which has since become one of the world's most cherished love songs. The vocal arrangement has a guitar part that features a combination of open and stopped strings in *campanella* style. The resultant harmonic effect is quite impressionistic at times.

Afton Water. There seem to be at least three popular versions of this song. Burns' melody is presented first. The second melody is by Alexander Hume (1811-59). It was probably written for Mrs General Stewart of Stair and Afton, on whose estate the stream of Afton Water is located. Afton Water is a tributary of the River Nith, which rises in East Ayrshire.

Corn Rigs. This is one of Burns' earlier works from his time at Lochlea Farm in 1782. Annie Rankine lived two miles away from Burns at the time, and would later claim that she was the *Annie* of the song. That might have been a ruse to increase trade at the inn that she ran. Corn rigs were a traditional drainage system used to divide fields into ridges around three feet high.

John Anderson My Jo. Burns took what was originally a bawdy song and transformed it into a ballad on the theme of eternal love. John Anderson was a carpenter in Ayrshire and a friend of Robert Burns.

My Nannie's Awa'. This song is generally sung to the traditional tune, *There are Few Good Fellows When Jamie's Awa'*. Although the ballad highlights the many joys that nature can offer, it seems that the lovesick young man can no longer find happiness, as he can only think about his departed lover.

Lord Gregory. Robert Burns made his own version of the traditional song, *Lord Gregory*, which according to the folksong collector Francis Childe, first appeared in print in the early Eighteenth Century. This song is from the perspective of a young woman jilted by Lord Gregory. It is clear that she has conceived a child out of wedlock by Lord Gregory, and that she has been disowned by her family.

My Love She's But A Lassie. In 1787, Burns was enlisted as a contributor to a collection of traditional Scottish songs called *The Scots Musical Museum*. He collected and revised many songs, of which this lively song was one. The music is taken from *Lady Badinscoth's Reel*.

A Man's A Man For A' That. This song, also known as Is *There for Honest Poverty* is an embodiment of Burns' egalitarian ideals derived from the vogue for liberalism in the Eighteenth Century. It found more recent fame when it was sung at the opening of the Scottish Parliament in 1999.

Comin' Thro' the Rye. This jaunty song was first written by Burns in 1782. It is, however, undoubtedly based on a much older melody and set of words. The original version, which told of a girl dragging her wet petticoat through the rye fields, was probably sanitised in the Victorian period.

Auld Lang Syne. This is the most famous of all New Year or Hogmanay songs, sung the world over. The second melody is the one that Burns originally intended, and it is slow and haunting in nature. It is thought to be an elaboration of an already existing complete song that began with the line *should auld acquaintance be forgot* and possibly dates back to the Sixteenth Century. The first, more popular melody, is known as *The Miller's Wedding* or *The Miller's Daughter*. It was first set to Burns' words in 1799. We will never know if Burns would have approved, but its popularity remains uncontested. The title roughly translates as *Old Time's Sake*.

O Lay Thy Loof. This love song was written by Burns for the sixth volume of the Musical Museum. The melody of the piece is entitled *The Cordwainer's March*, cordwainers being shoemakers. *Loof* is the Old Scots word for palm.

Ae Fond Kiss. This is Burns' most recorded love song. It started life in a letter sent to a female friend of Burns, Mrs Agnes Maclehose, who he had promised to marry (despite being married to Jean Armour at the time!). Again, the melody that we know and love is not the one intended by Burns, but a completely different gaelic air.

The Soldier's Return. This multi-versed song tells of the return of a soldier from combat. His sweetheart does recognise him at first, but tells him that she has inherited her grandfather's estate and wants to share it with him. The song ends with a plea to honour *the brave poor sodger*. The mill mentioned in the second verse is in Kilmannoch and is still standing.

The Weary Pund O' Tow. This song was first published in the fourth volume of the Musical Museum. Its melody remains unchanged, and may have originated in a 1759 book entitled *The Pocket Caledonian Companion*. The words, which may be based on an earlier ballad, concern a husband who laments his wife's lack of housework. His wife does not respond well to criticism and clouts him over the head with a rock!

My Heart's In the Highlands. This song was first printed in The Scots Musical Museum paired with a Gaelic Air called *Failte na moisg*. However, this version, based upon another air called *Crochallan*, has become very popular. It tells of Burns' love of the Scottish outdoors. According to Burns, *the first half of the first stanza is old – the rest is mine.*

Mary Morison. There is a gravestone in the churchyard of Mauchline, East Ayrshire that bears the Inscription: *In memory of Adjutant John Morison, etc, etc.; also his daughter - the poet's bonnie Mary Morison - who died 29th June, 1791, aged 20.* Mary died of either septicaemia or consumption. It is possible, however, that the song was really about Alison Begbie, who rejected the marriage proposal of Robert Burns when he was twenty three years of age.

Ye Banks and Braes. This tune was written in 1778 by Charles Miller, as a challenge to write an authentic Scottish air. The melody was passed to Burns, whose words refer to the *bonnie Doon*, which is a river that passes through Burns' home town of Alloway, Ayrshire.

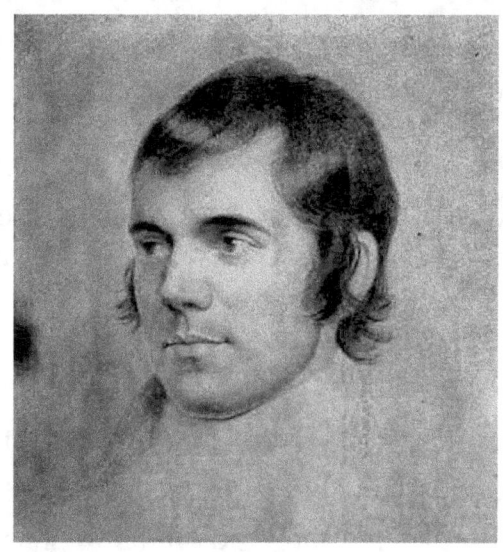

Robert Burns by Archibald Skirving, 1796

Robert Burns Songs
Arranged for Guitar and Voice

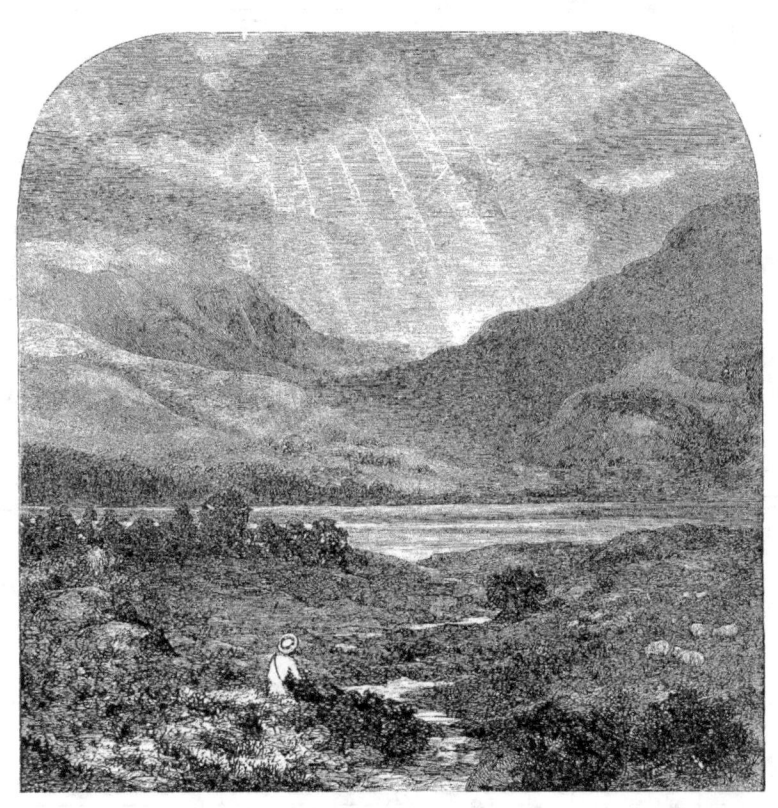

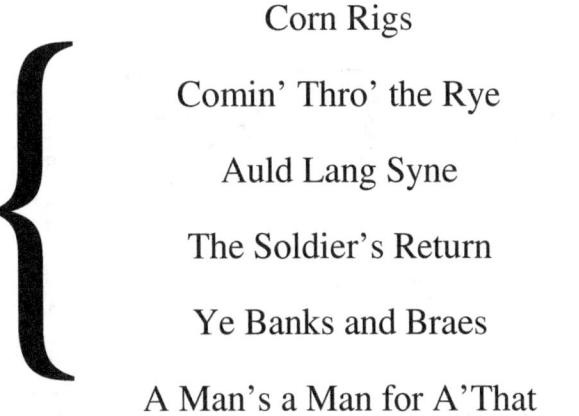

Corn Rigs

Comin' Thro' the Rye

Auld Lang Syne

The Soldier's Return

Ye Banks and Braes

A Man's a Man for A' That

Can also be played by

flute or recorder

My Love Is Like a Red, Red Rose

Robert Burns

Traditional

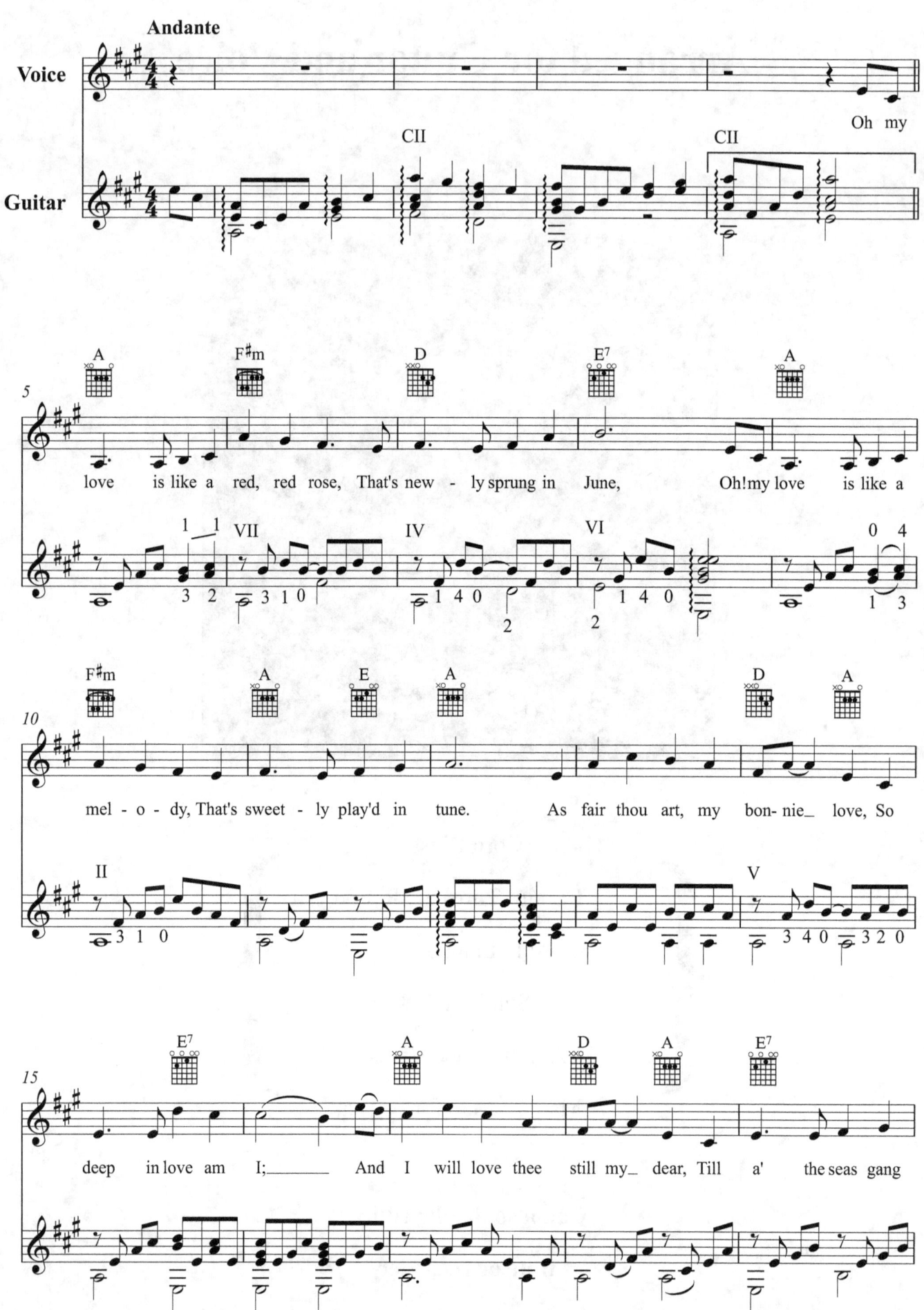

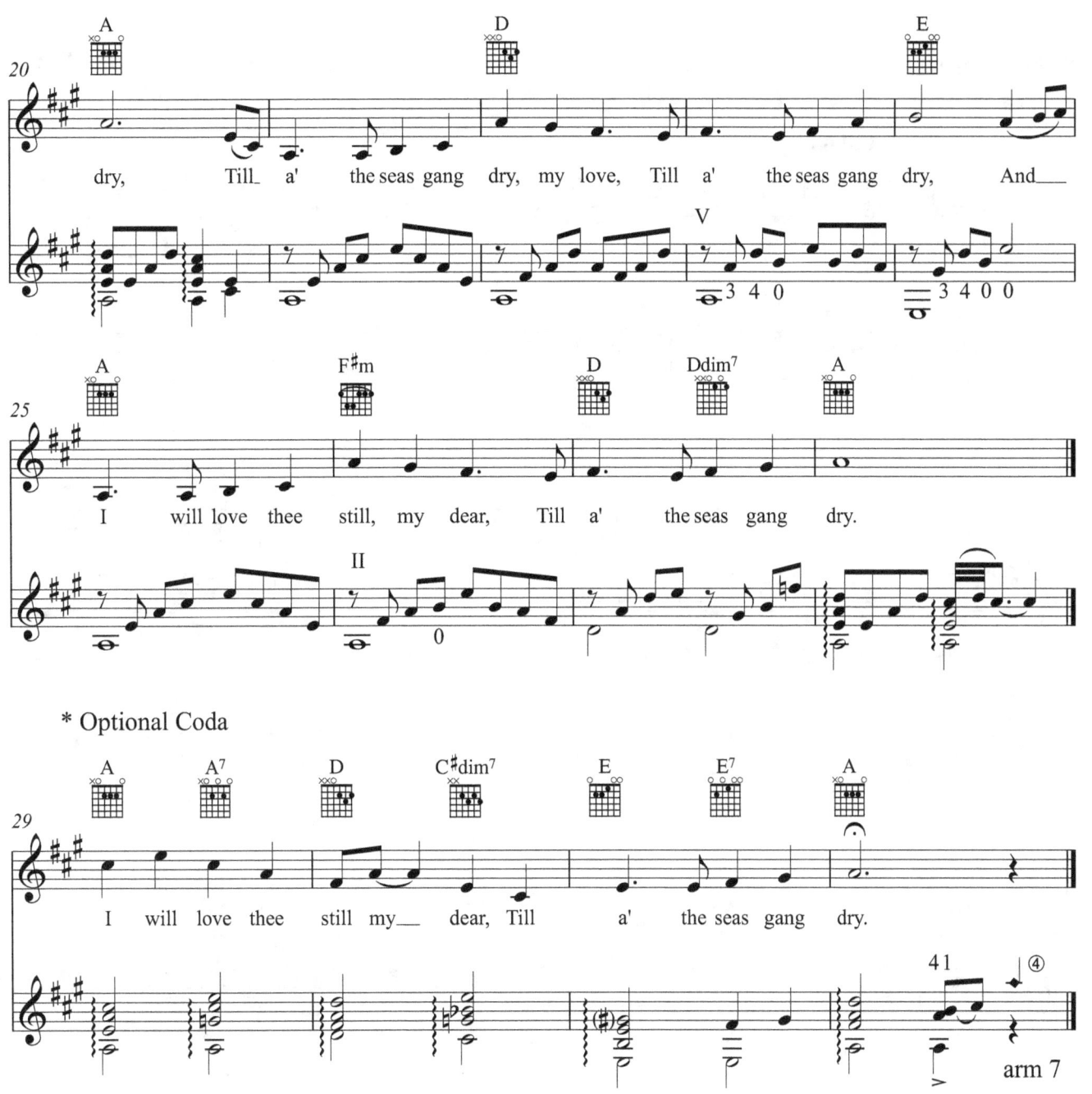

* Optional Coda

Till a' the seas gang dry, my dear,
And the rocks melt wi' the sun;
And I will love thee still, my dear,
While the sands o' life shall run.

And fare thee weel, my only love!
And fare thee weel a while;
And I will come again, my love,
Tho' 'twere ten thousand mile.

Afton Water (Original Version)

Robert Burns

Traditional

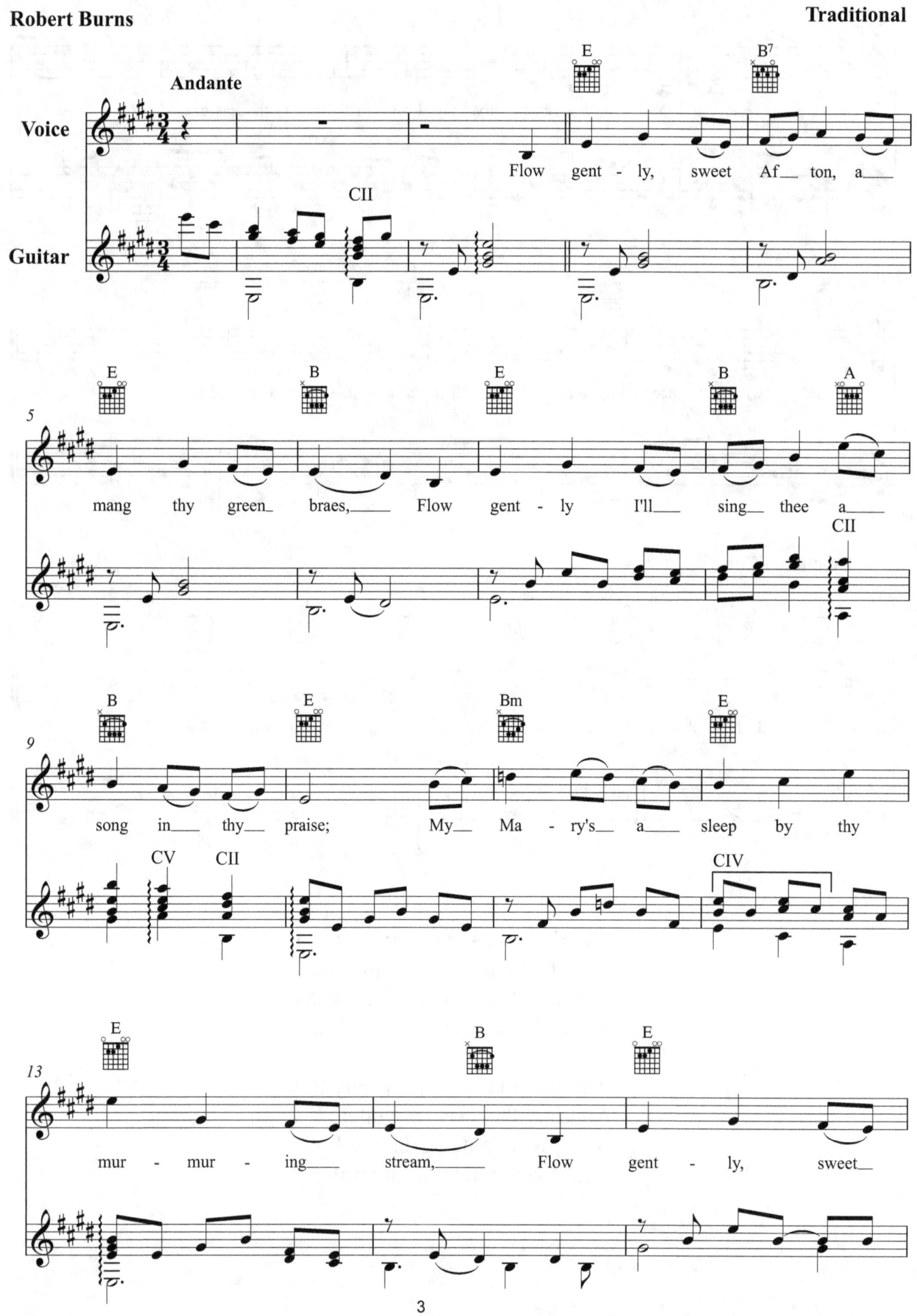

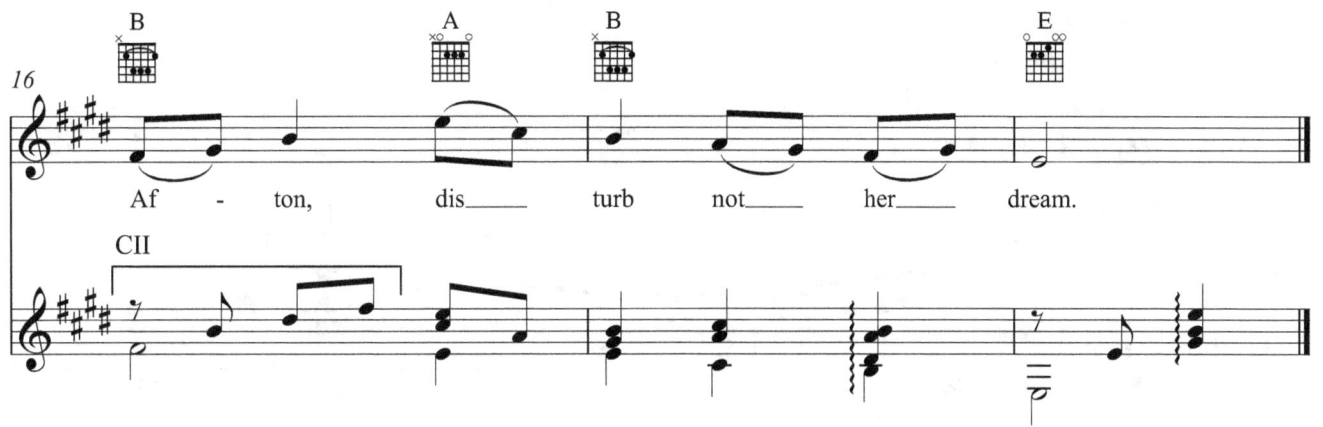

Af - ton, dis___ turb not___ her___ dream.

Thou stock dove whose echo resounds thro' the glen,
Ye wild whistling blackbirds in yon thorny den,
Thou green-crested lapwing, thy screaming forbear
I charge you, disturb not my slumbering fair!

How lofty, sweet Afton, thy neighbouring hills,
Far marked with the courses of clear, winding rills,
There daily I wander, as noon rises high,
My flocks and my Mary's sweet cot in my eye.

How pleasant thy banks and green valleys below,
Where wild in the woodlands the primroses blow,
There oft, as mild evening weeps over the lea,
The sweet-scented birk shades my Mary and me.

Thy crystal stream, Afton, how lovely it glides,
And winds by the cot where my Mary resides;
How wanton thy waters her snowy feet lave,
As, gathering sweet flowerets, she stems thy clear wave.

Flow gently, sweet Afton, among thy green braes,
Flow gently, sweet river, the theme of my lays;
My Mary's asleep by thy murmuring stream,
Flow gently, sweet Afton, disturb not her dream.

Afton Water

Robert Burns

Alexander Hume

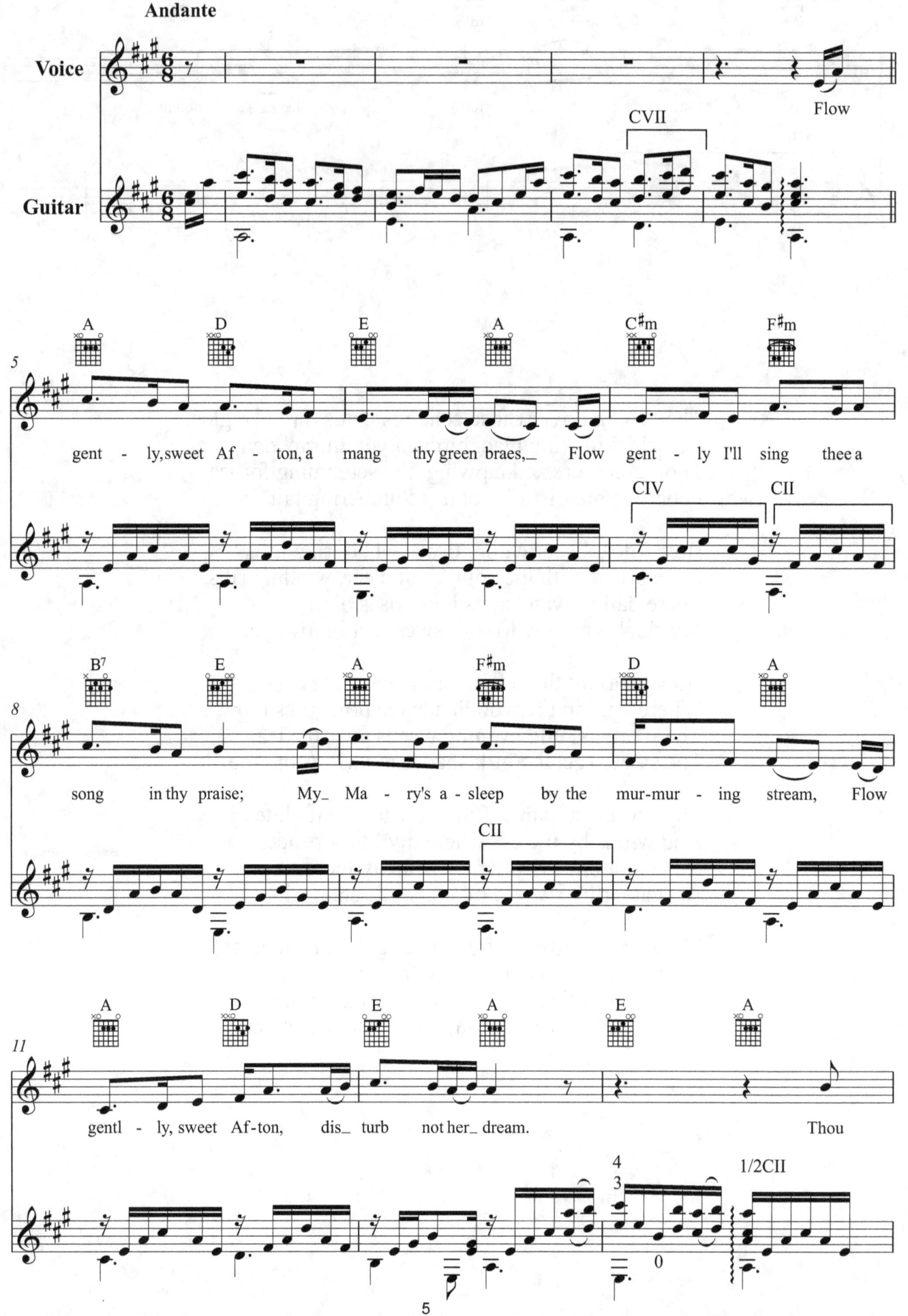

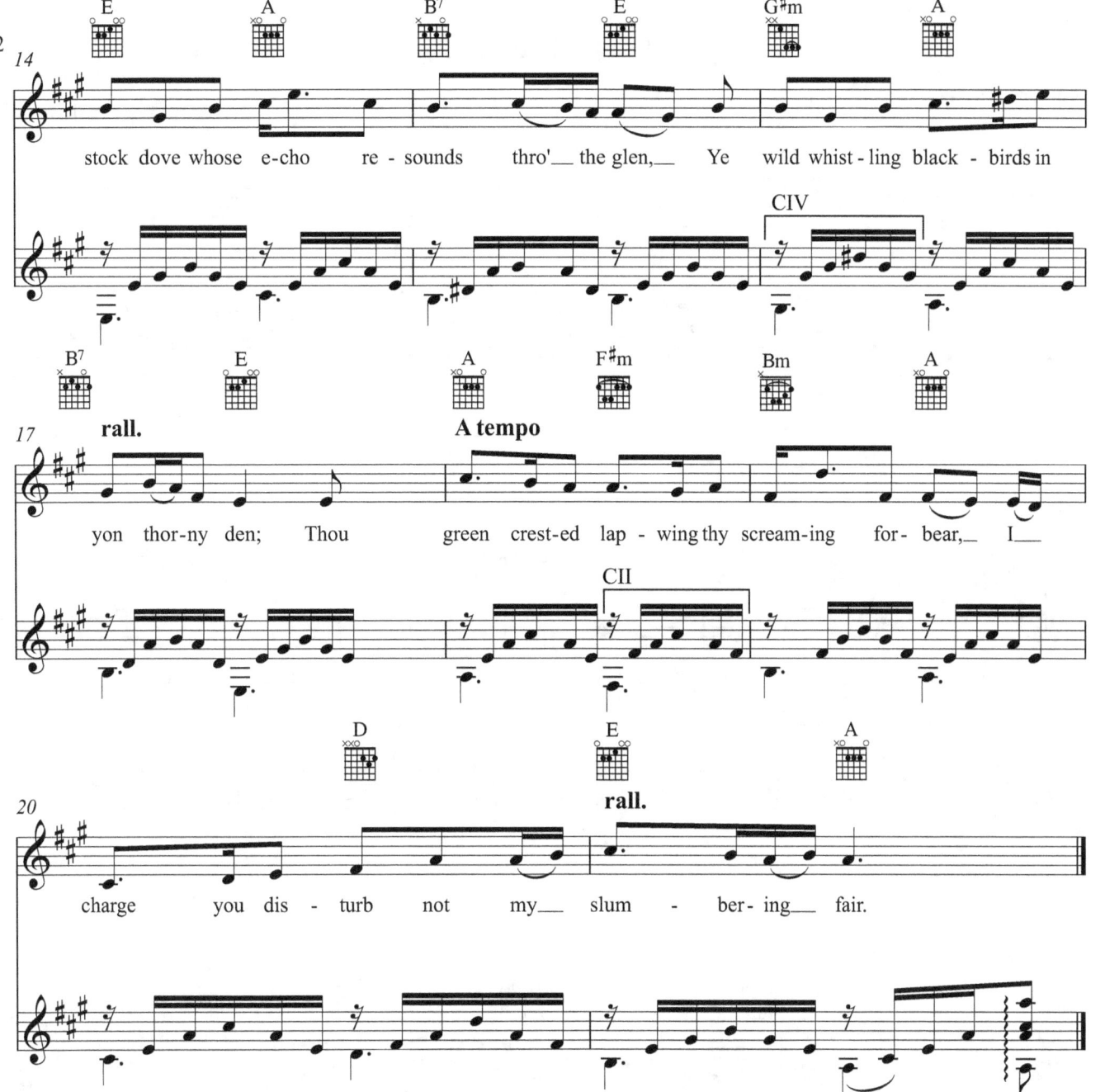

How lofty, sweet Afton, thy neighbouring hills,
Far marked with the courses of clear winding rills;
There daily I wander as noon rises high,
My flocks and my Mary's sweet cot in my eye.

How pleasant thy banks and green valleys below,
Where wild in the woodlands the primroses blow;
There oft, as mild evening sweeps over the lea,
The sweet-scented birk shades my Mary and me.

Thy crystal stream, Afton, how lovely it glides,
And winds by the cot where my Mary resides,
How wanton thy waters her snowy feet lave,
As gathering sweet flowerets she stems thy clear wave.

Flow gently, sweet Afton, among thy green braes,
Flow gently, sweet river, the theme of my lays;
My Mary's asleep by thy murmuring stream,
Flow gently, sweet Afton, disturb not her dream.

Corn Rigs

Robert Burns

Traditional

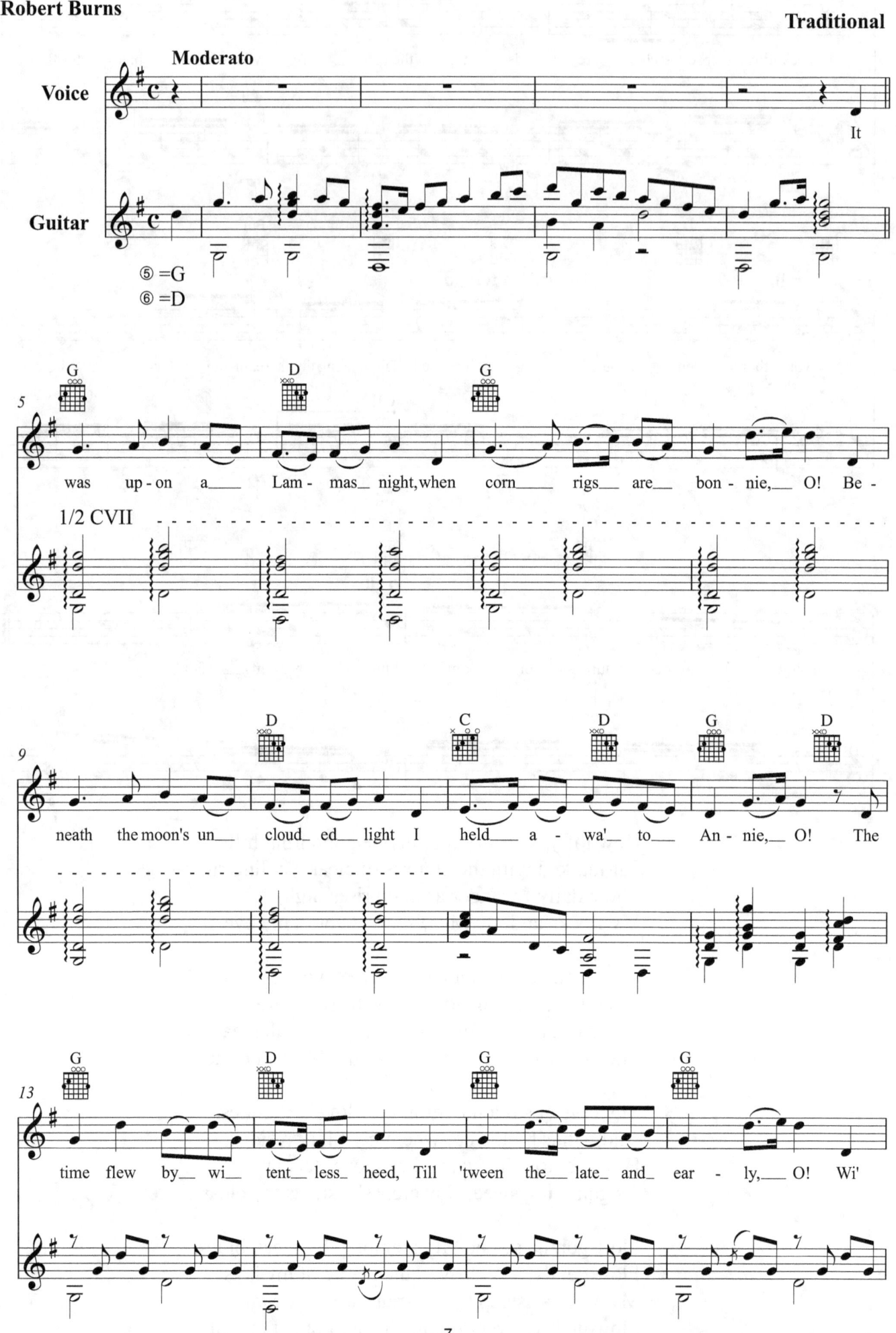

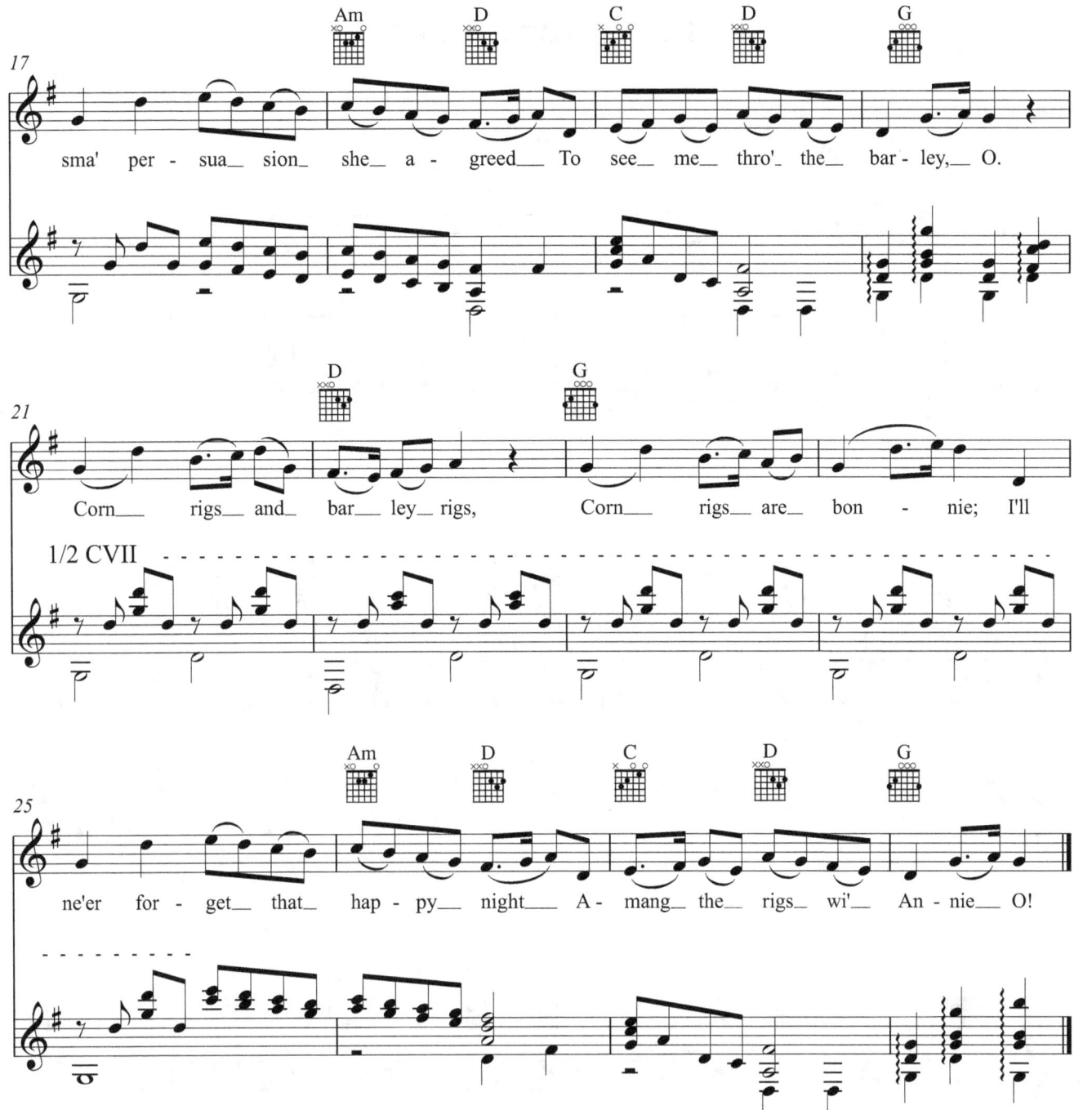

The sky was blue, the wind was still, The moon was shining clearly, O!
I set her down, wi' right good will, Amang the rigs o' barley, O!
I kent her heart was a' my ain; I lov'd her most sincerely, O!
I kiss'd her owre and owre again, Amang the rigs o' barley, O!

Corn rigs, etc.

I locked her in my fond embrace; Her heart was beating rarely, O!
My blessings on that happy place, Amang the rigs o' barley, O!
But by the moon and stars so bright, That shone that hour so clearly, O!
She aye shall bless that happy night, Amang the rigs o' barley, O.

Corn rigs, etc.

I hae been blythe wi' comrades dear; I hae been merry drinkin', O!
I hae been joyfu' gath'rin' gear; I hae been happy thinkin', O!
But a' the pleasures e'er I saw, Tho' three times doubled fairly, O!
That happy night was worth them a', Amang the rigs o' barley, O.

Corn rigs, etc.

John Anderson, my Jo

Traditional

Robert Burns

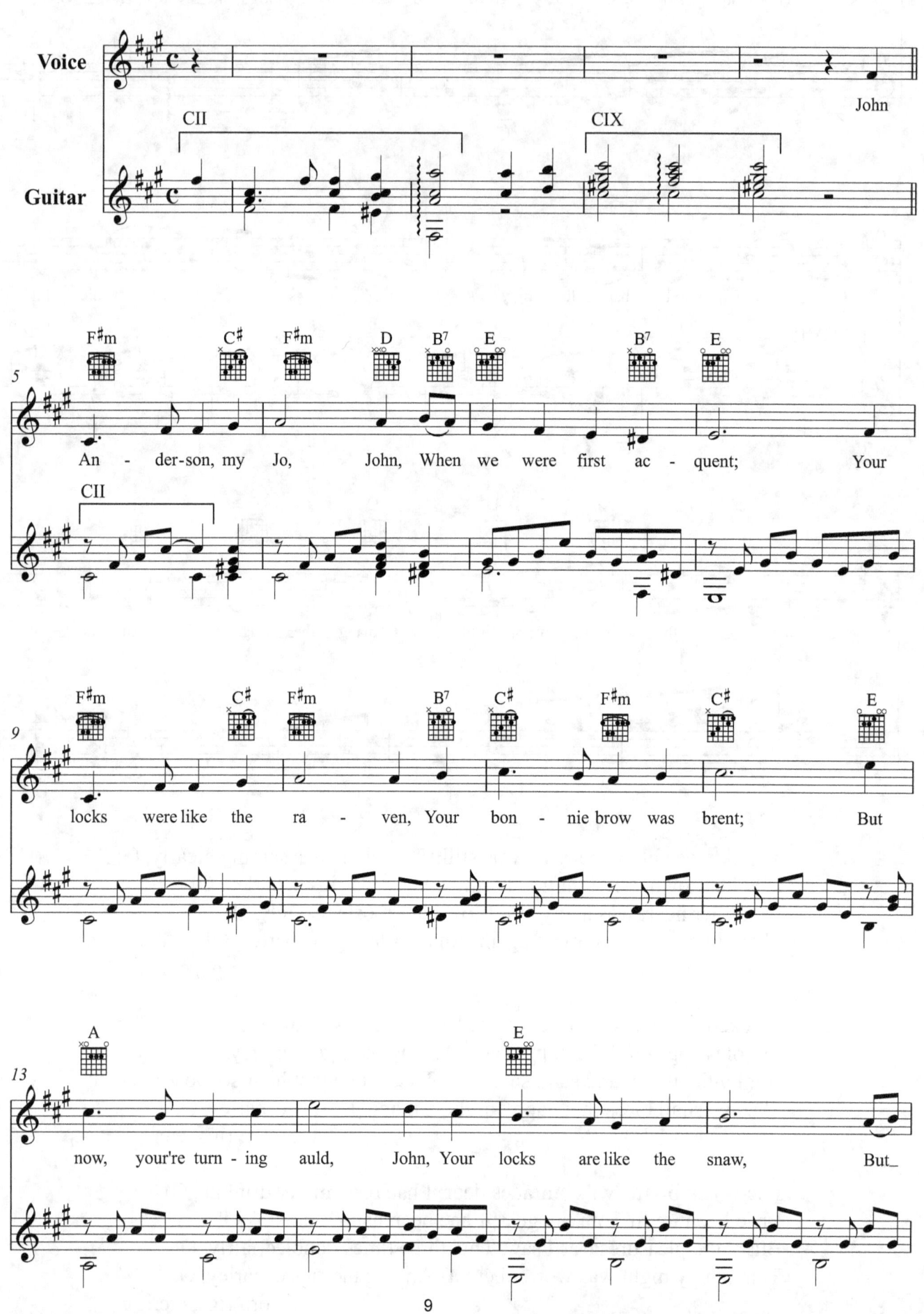

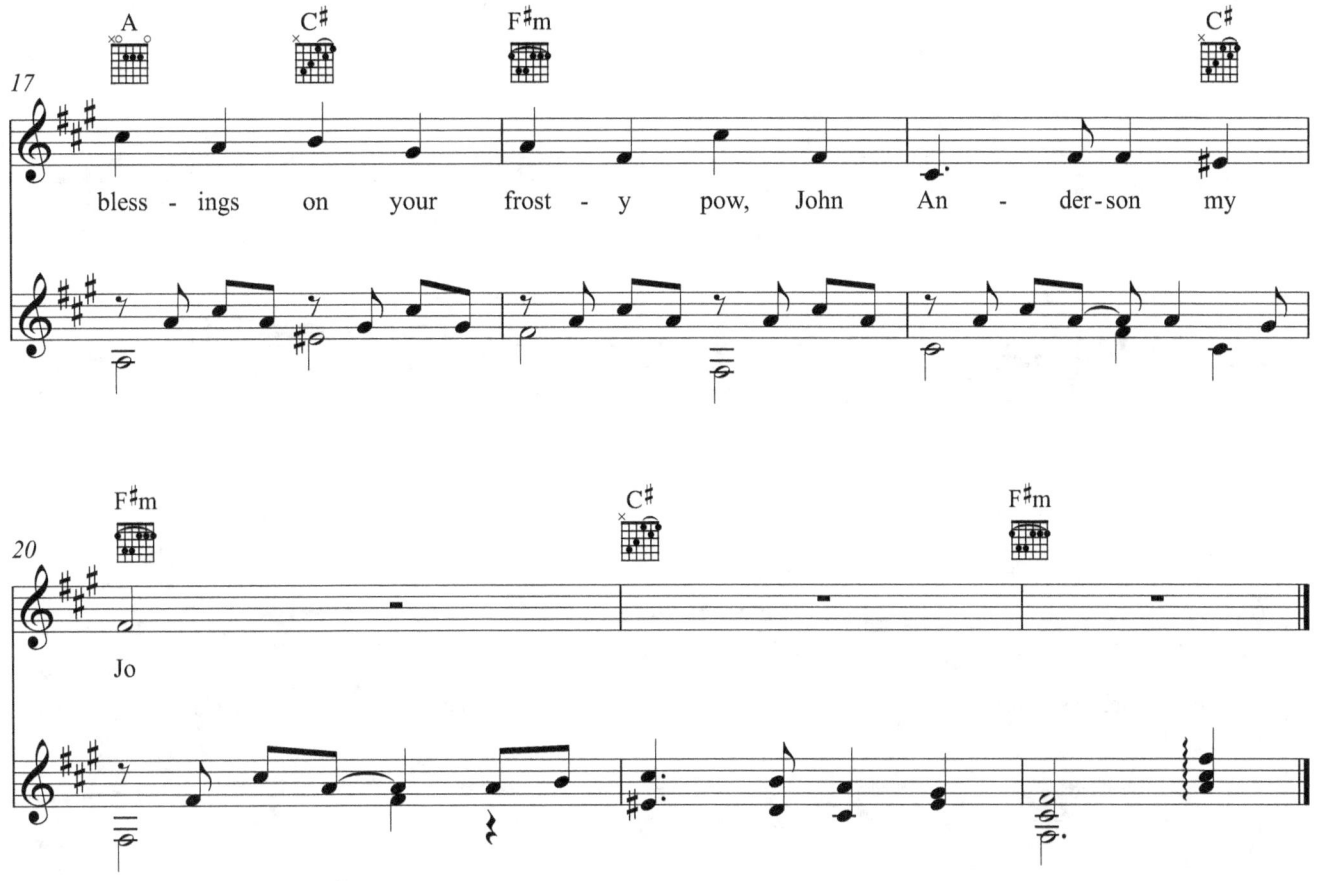

John Anderson my Jo, John,
We clamb the hill thegither,
And mony a cantie day, John,
We've had wi' ane anither;
Now we maun totter down, John,
But hand in hand we'll go,
And sleep thegither at the foot,
John Anderson, my Jo.

My Nannie's Awa'!

Robert Burns

Traditional

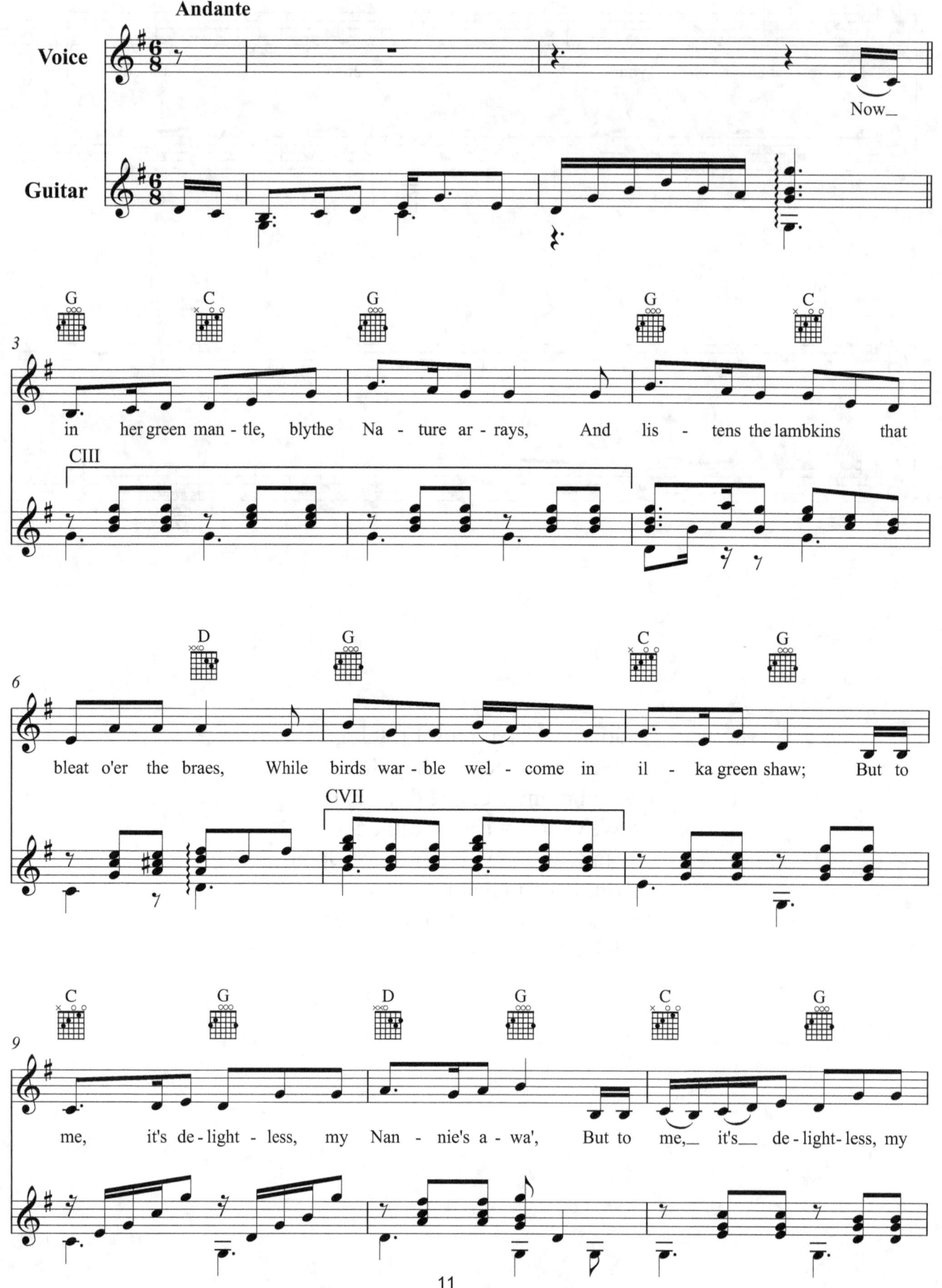

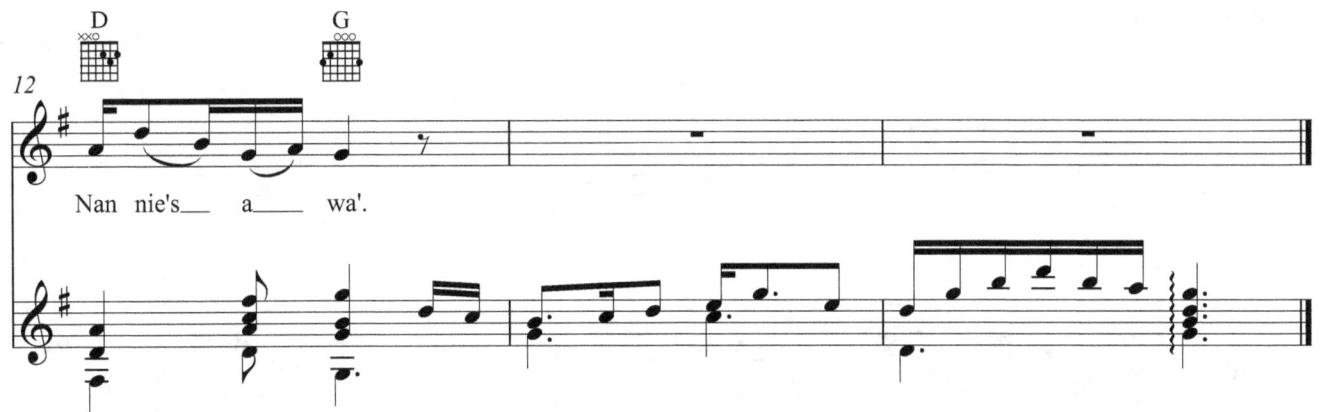

Nan nie's___ a___ wa'.

The snow-drop and primrose our woodlands adorn,
And violets bathe in the weet o' the morn;
They pain my sad bosom, sae sweetly they blaw!
They mind me o' Nannie - and Nannie's awa'.

Thou laverock, that springs frae the dews o' the lawn,
The shepherd to warn of the grey-breakin' dawn,
And thou mellow mavis, that hails the night-fa';
Give over for pity - my Nannie's awa'.

Come, autumn, sae pensive, in yellow and grey,
And soothe me wi' tidings o' Nature's decay;
The dark, dreary winter, and wild-driving snaw,
Alone can delight me - my Nannie's awa'.

Lord Gregory

Robert Burns

Traditional

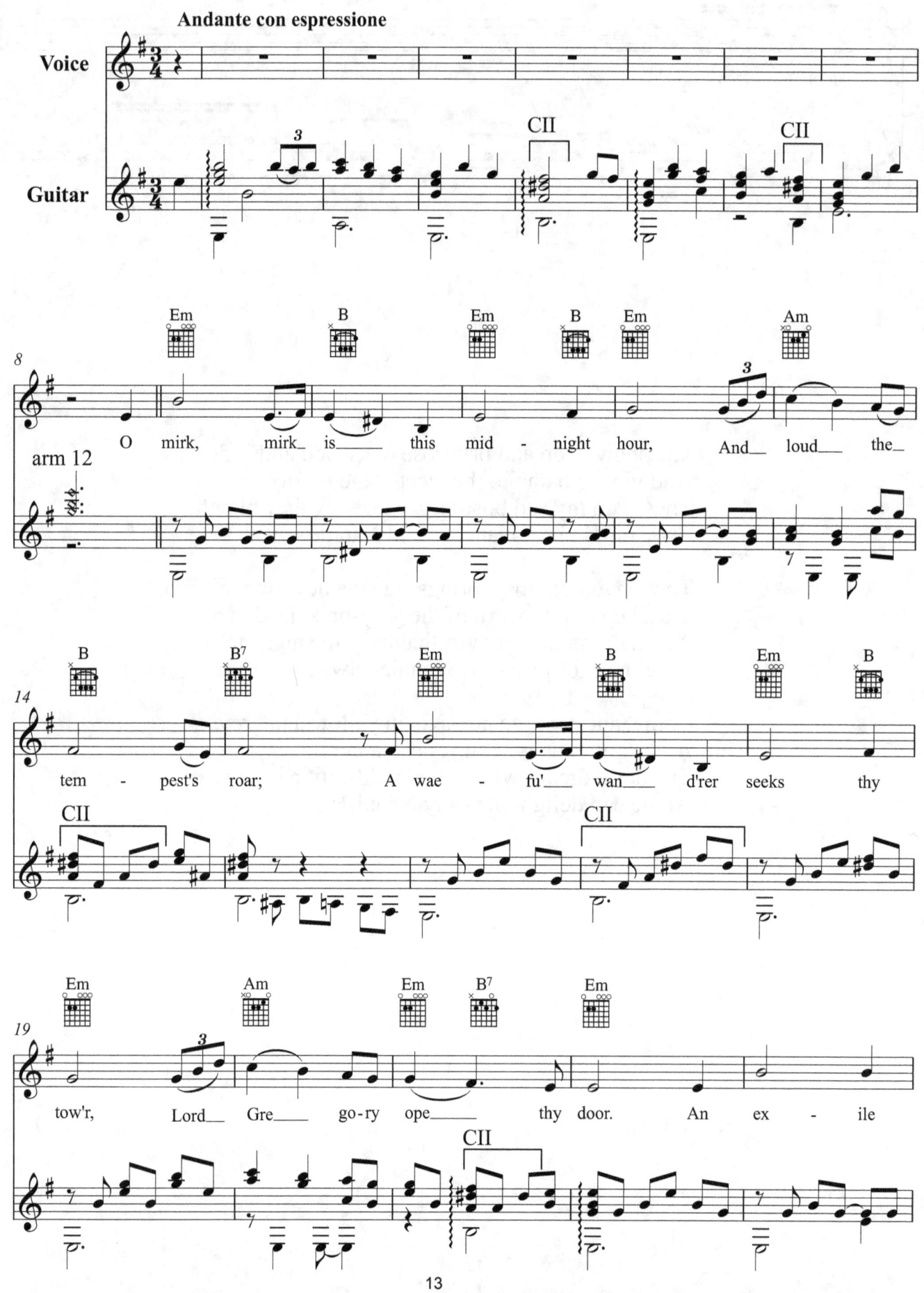

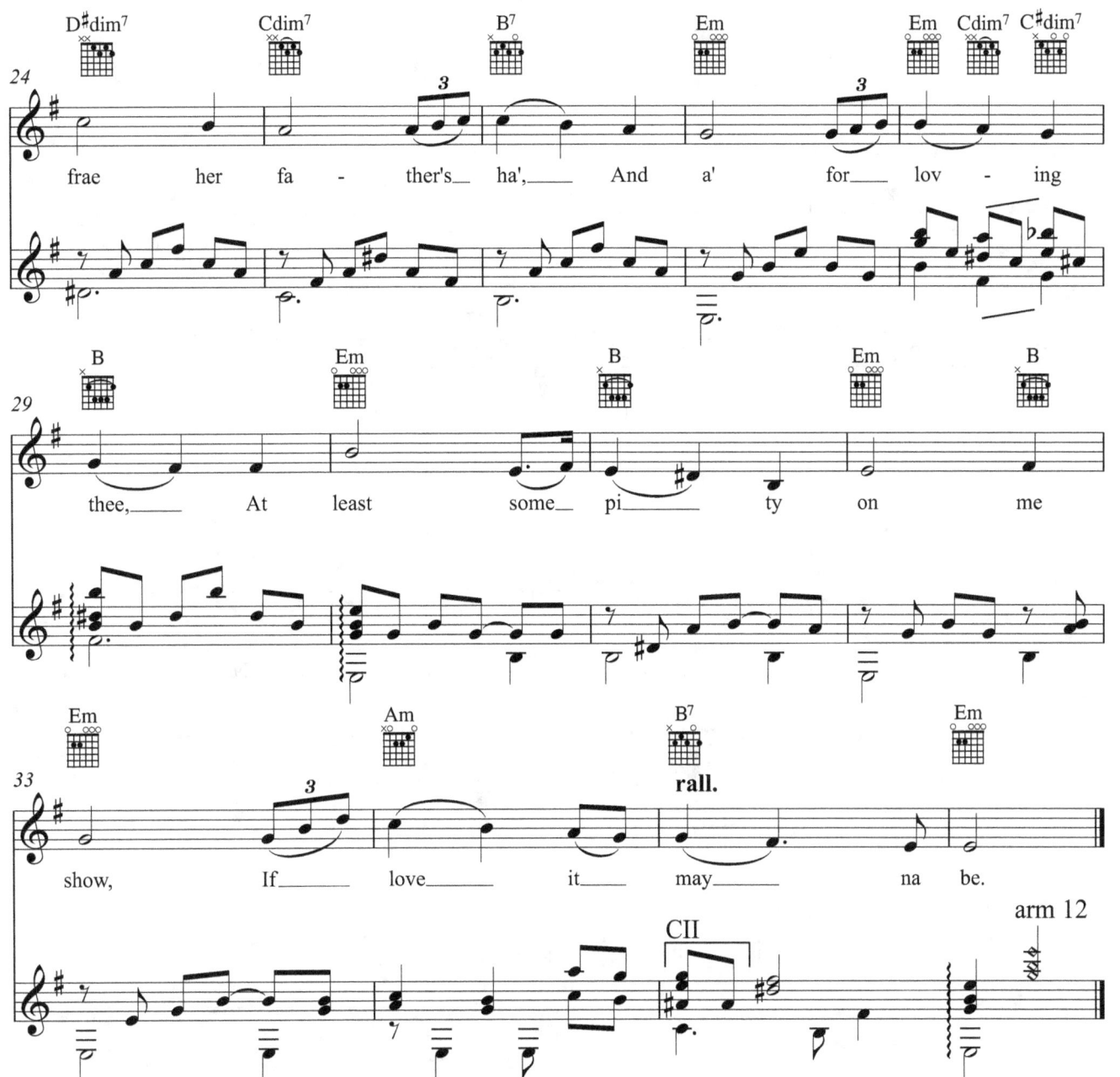

Lord Gregory, mind'st thou not the grove,
By bonnie Irvine-side,
Where first I own'd that virgin-love,
I lang, lang had denied?
How aften didst thou pledge and vow,
Thou wad for aye be mine!
And my fond heart, itsel sae true,
It ne'er mistrusted thine.

Hard is thy heart, Lord Gregory,
And flinty is thy breast:
Thou dart of heaven that flashest by,
O wilt thou give me rest!
Ye mustering thunders from above,
Your willing victim see!
But spare, and pardon my fause love,
His wrangs to heaven and me!

14

My Love She's But A Lassie

Robert Burns

Traditional

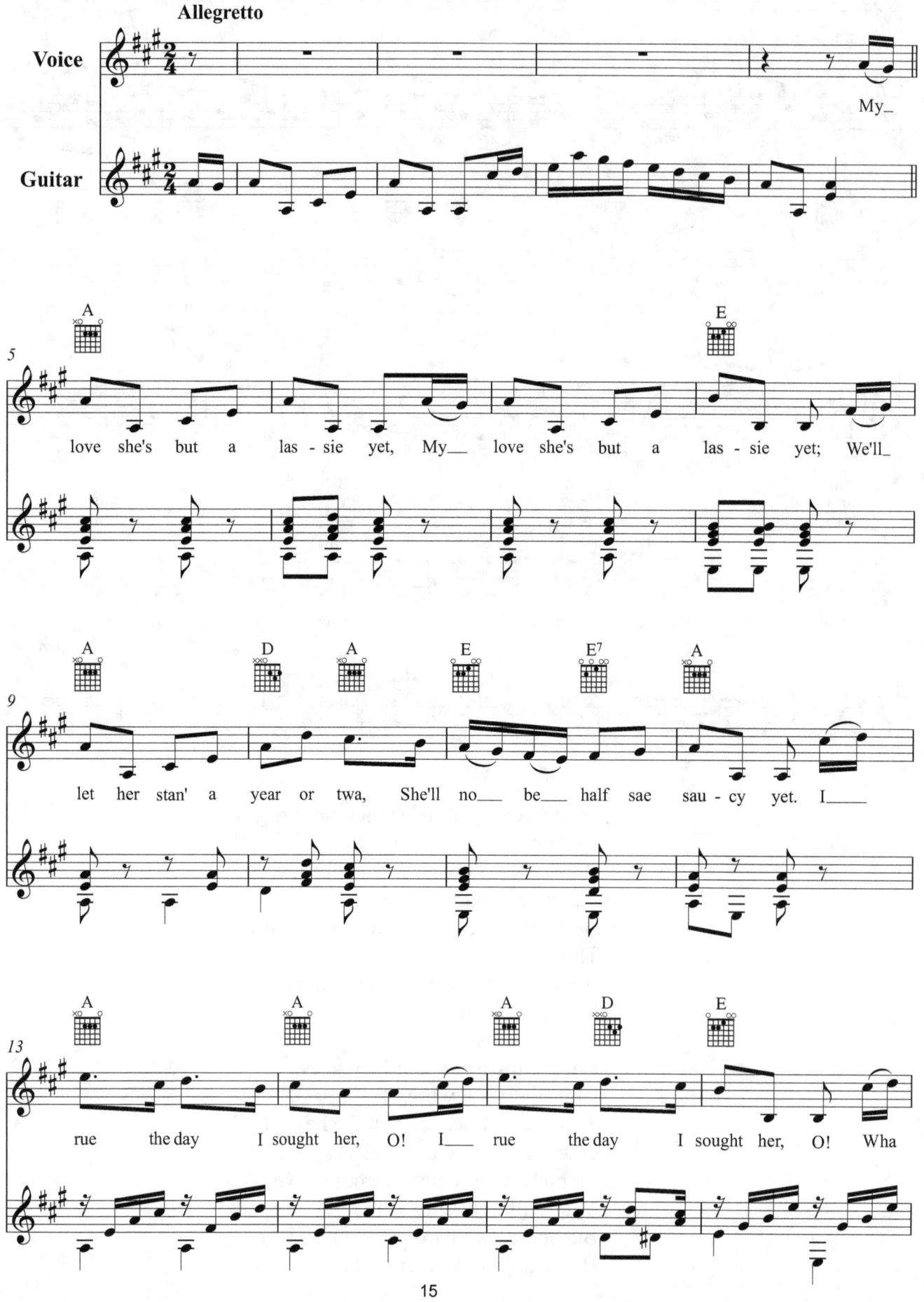

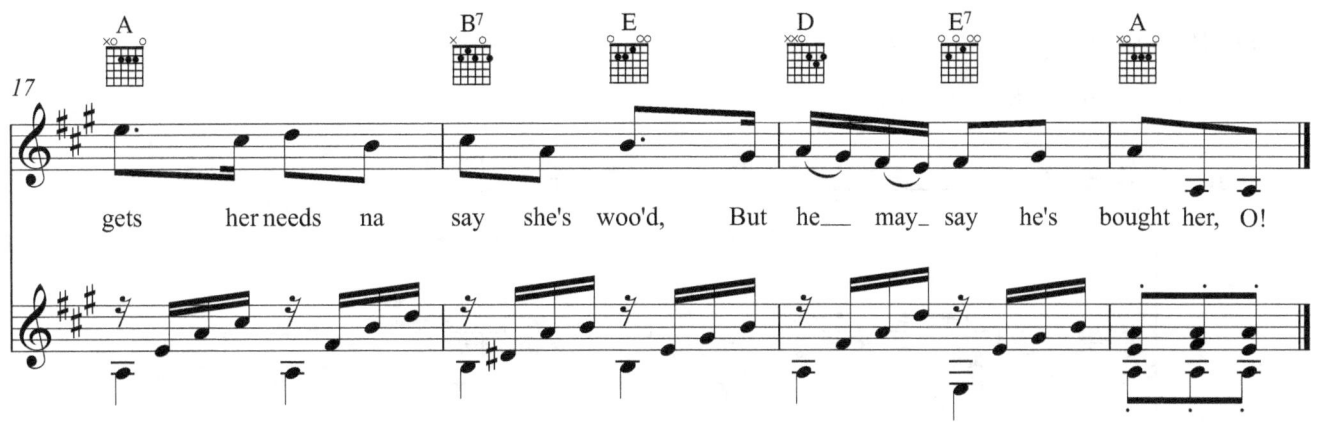

gets her needs na say she's woo'd, But he__ may_ say he's bought her, O!

Come, draw a drap o' the best o't yet;
Come, draw a drap o' the best o't yet;
Gae seek for pleasure where ye will,
But here I never miss'd it yet.
We're a' dry wi' drinkin o't,
We're a' dry wi' drinkin o't;
The minister kiss'd the fiddler's wife,
An' could na preach for thinkin o't.

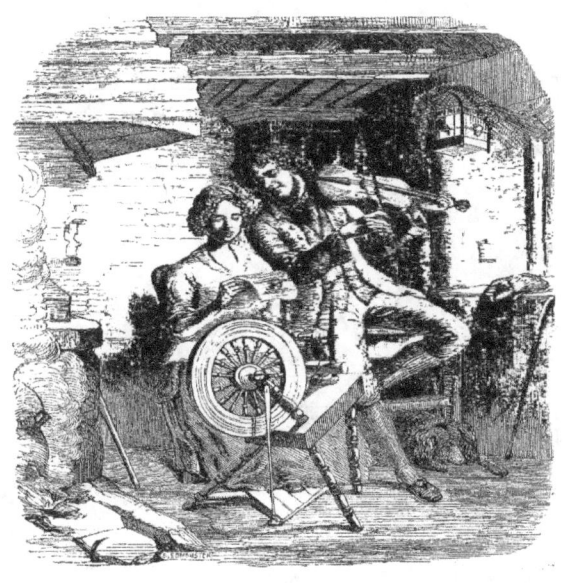

A Man's a Man for A' That

Traditional

Robert Burns

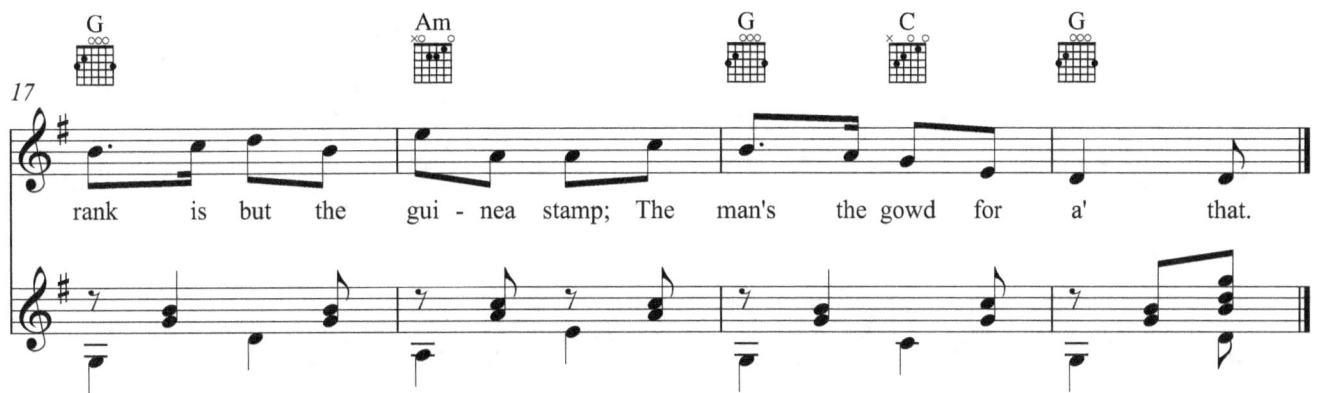

rank is but the gui - nea stamp; The man's the gowd for a' that.

What tho' on hamely fare we dine,
Wear hodden-grey, an' a that;
Gi'e fools their silks, and knaves their wine,
A man's a man for a' that.
For a' that, and a' that,
Their tinsel show, and a' that;
The honest man, tho' e'er sae poor,
Is king o' men for a' that.

Ye see yon birkie, ca'd a lord,
Wha struts, and stares, and a' that;
Tho' hundreds worship at his word,
He's but a coof for a' that:
For a' that, and a' that,
His ribband, star, and a' that,
The man of independent mind
He looks and laughs at a' that.

A prince can mak a belted knight,
A marquis, duke, and a' that;
But an honest man's aboon his might,
Guid faith, he maunna fa' that!
For a' that, and a' that,
Their dignities and a' that,
The pith o' sense, and pride o' worth,
Are higher rank than a' that.

Then let us pray that come it may,
As come it will, for a' that;
That sense and worth, o'er a' the earth,
May bear the gree, an' a' that.
For a' that, and a' that,
It's coming yet, for a' that,
That man to man, the world o'er,
Shall brithers be for a' that.

Comin' Thro' The Rye

Robert Burns

Traditional

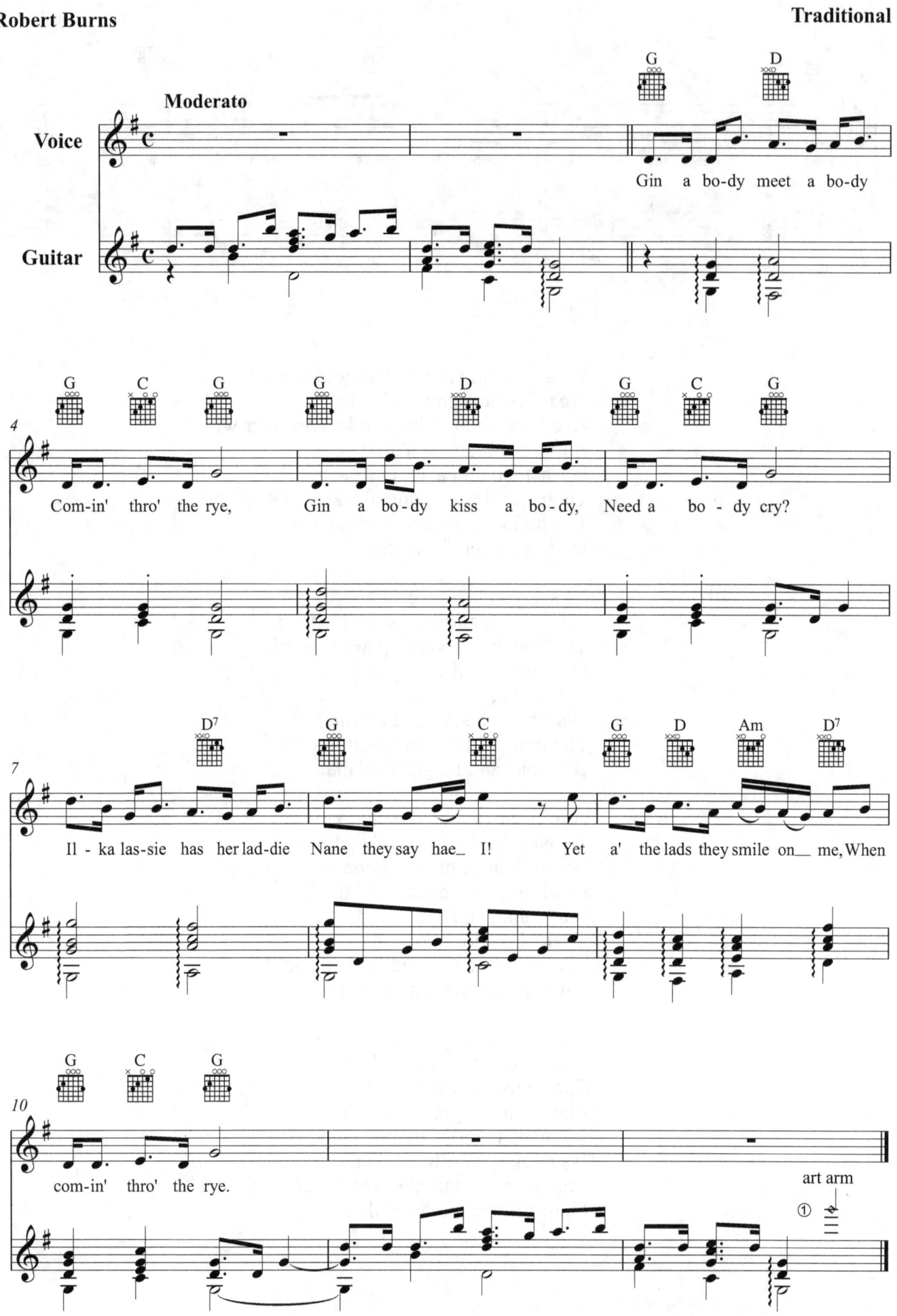

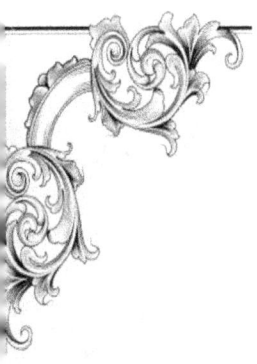
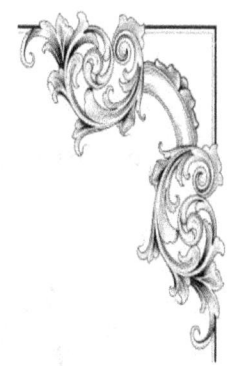

Gin a body meet a body
Comin' frae the well,
Gin a body kiss a body,
Need a body tell?
Ilka lassie has her laddie,
Ne'er a ane hae I!
But a' the lads they smile at me
When comin' thro' the rye.

Gin a body meet a body
Comin' frae the town,
Gin a body greet a body,
Need a body frown?
Ilka lassie has her laddie,
Nane they say hae I!
But a' the lads they lo'e me weel,
And what the waur am I?

Amang the train there is a swain
I dearly lo'e mysel',
But whaur his hame, or what his name,
I dinna care to tell!
Ilka lassie has her laddie,
Nane they say hae I!
But a' the lads they lo'e me weel,
And what the waur am I?

Auld Lang Syne

Robert Burns   **Traditional**

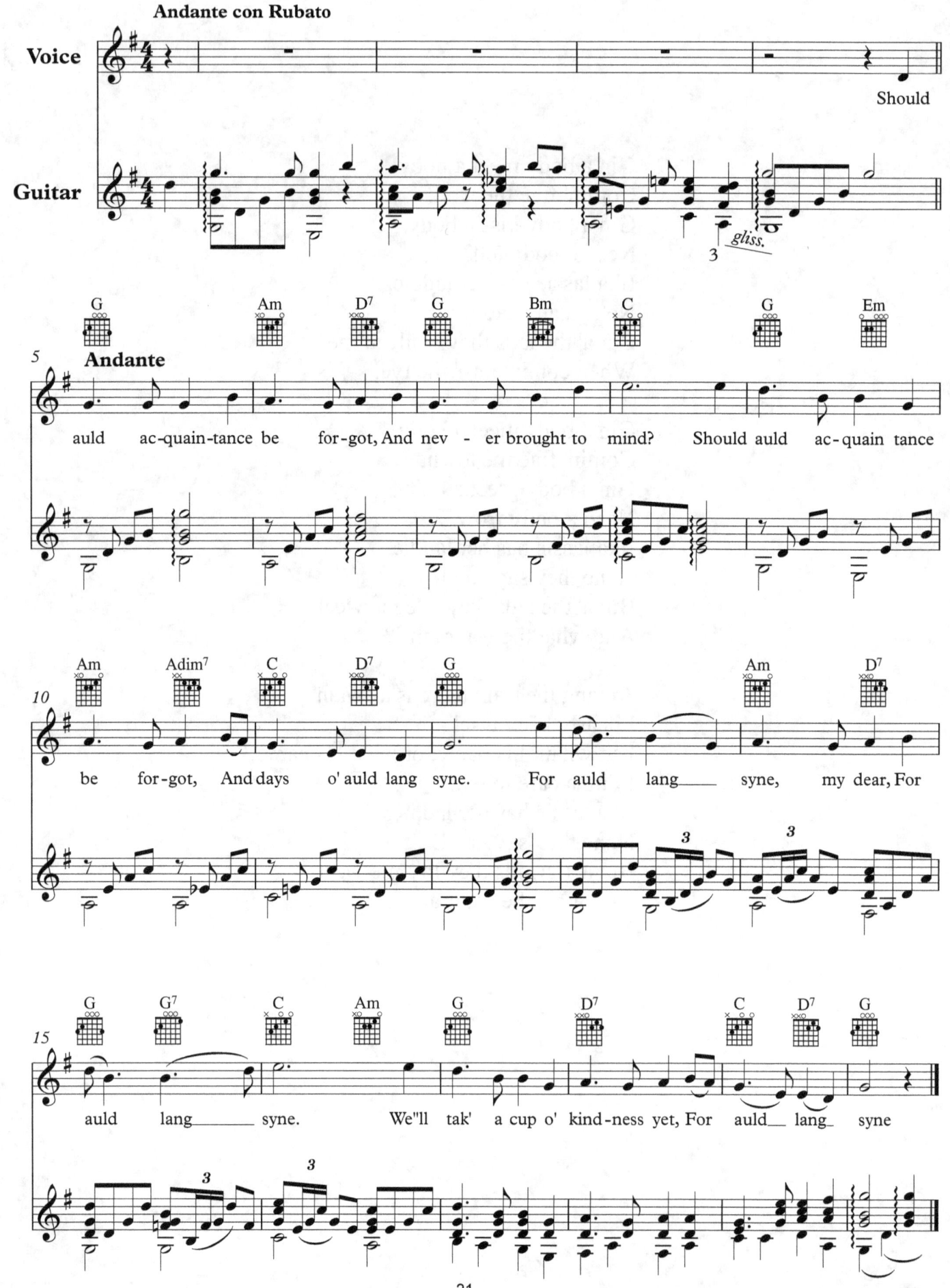

Auld Lang Syne (Original Version)

Robert Burns

Traditional

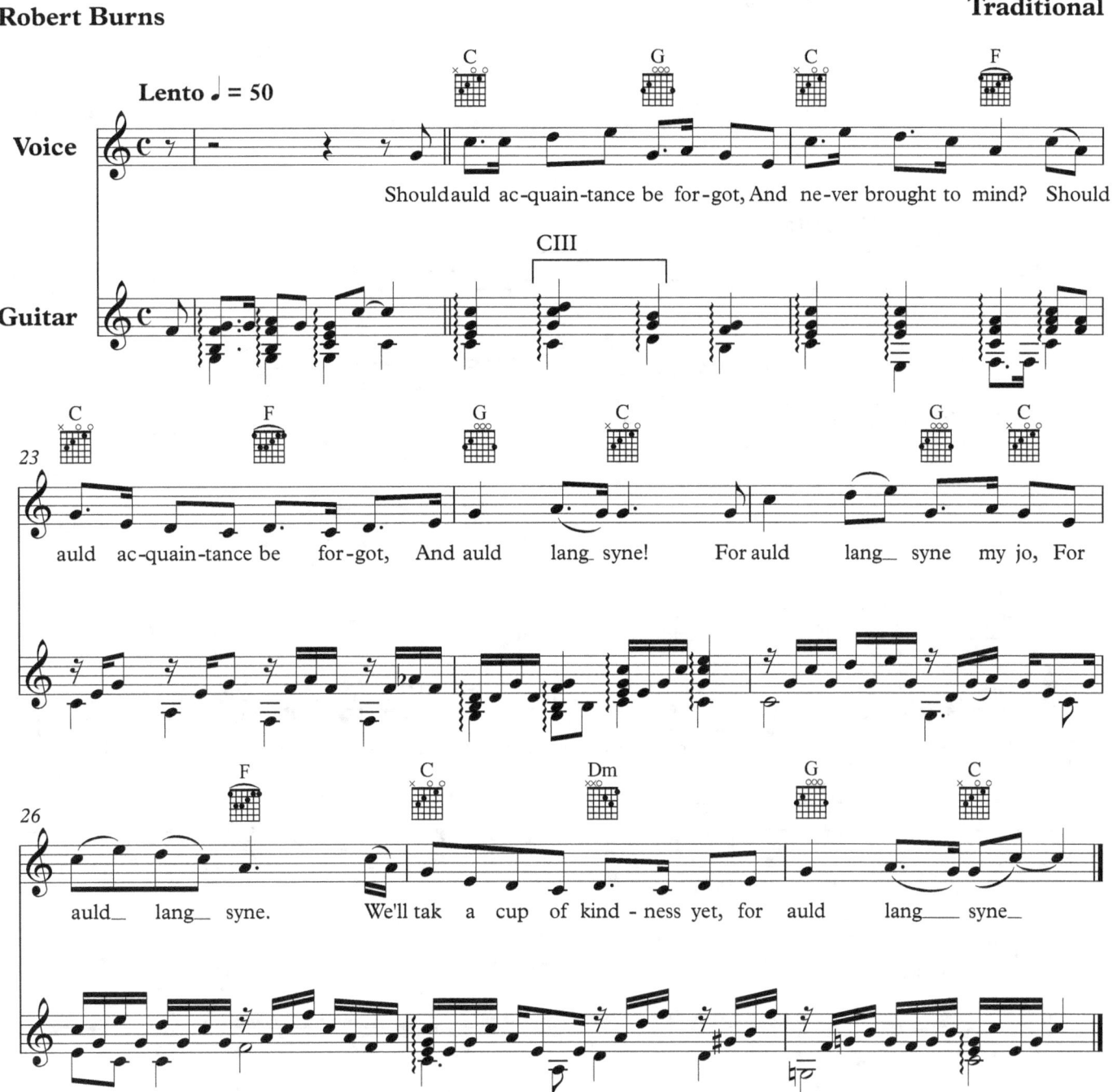

We twa hae run about the braes,
And pu'd the gowans fine,
But we've wander'd mony a weary foot
Sin' auld lang syne.

We twa hae paidl't in the burn
Frae morning sun till dine,
But seas between us braid hae roar'd
Sin' auld lang syne.

And there's a hand, my trusty fiere,
And gie's a hand o' thine,
And we'll tak a right guid willie-waught
For auld lang syne!

And surely ye'll be your pint' stoup,
And surely I'll be mine!
And we'll tak a cup o' kindness yet
For auld lang syne!

O Lay Thy Loof In Mine, Lass

Robert Burns

Traditional

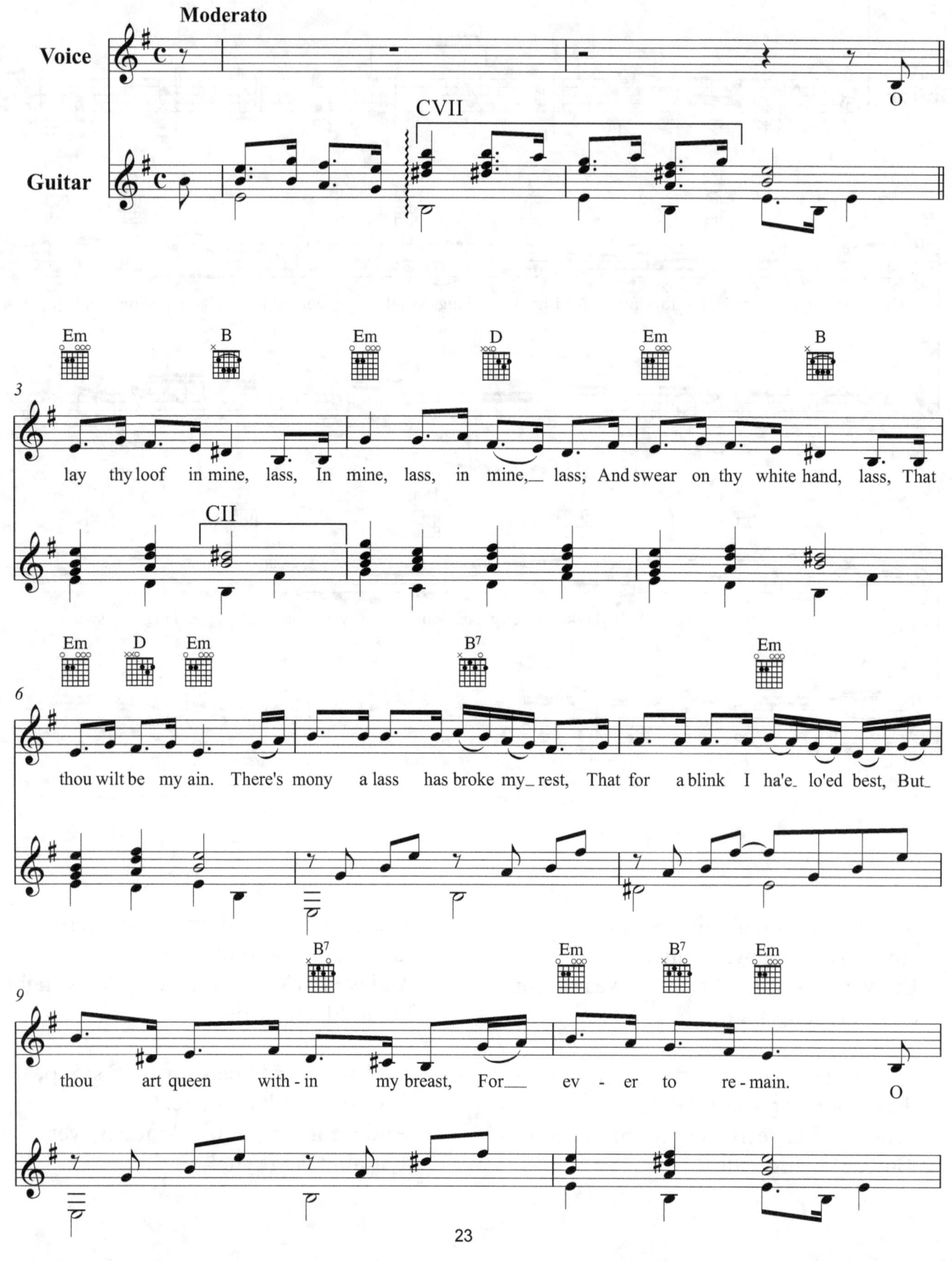

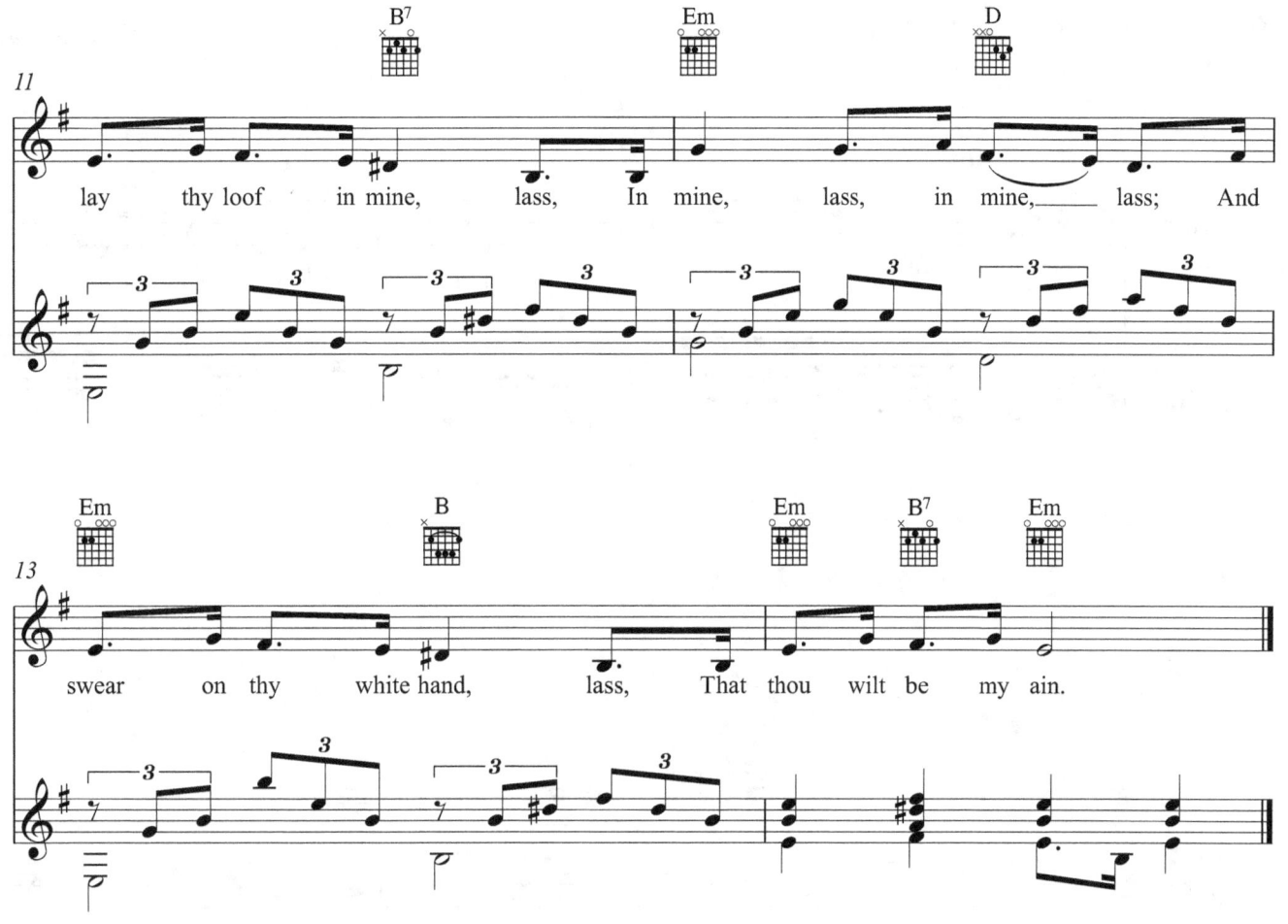

A slave to love's unbounded sway,
He aft has wrought me meikle wae;
But now he is my deadly fae,
Unless thou'lt be my ain.

                 O lay thy loof etc.

Ae Fond Kiss

Robert Burns

Traditional

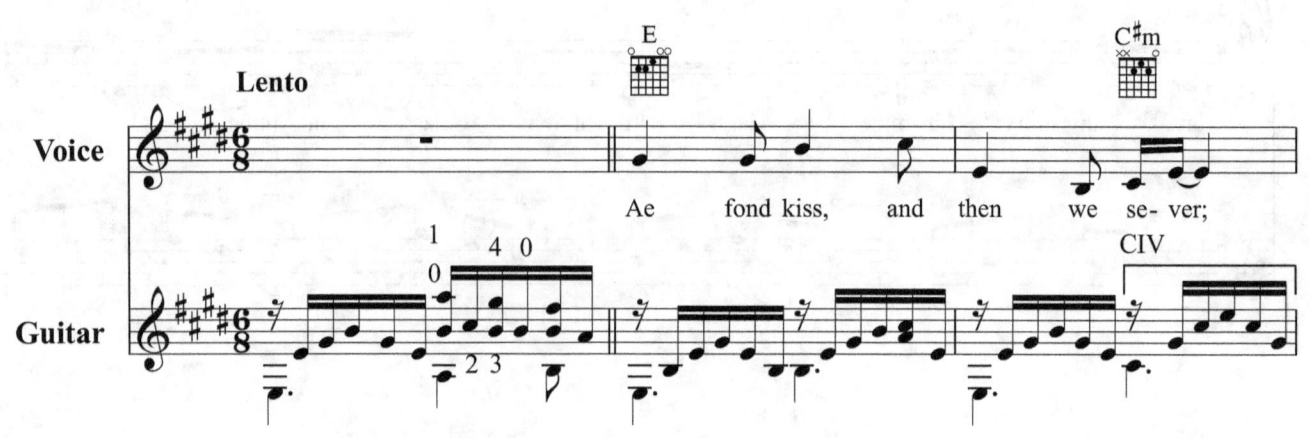

Ae fond kiss, and then we se- ver;

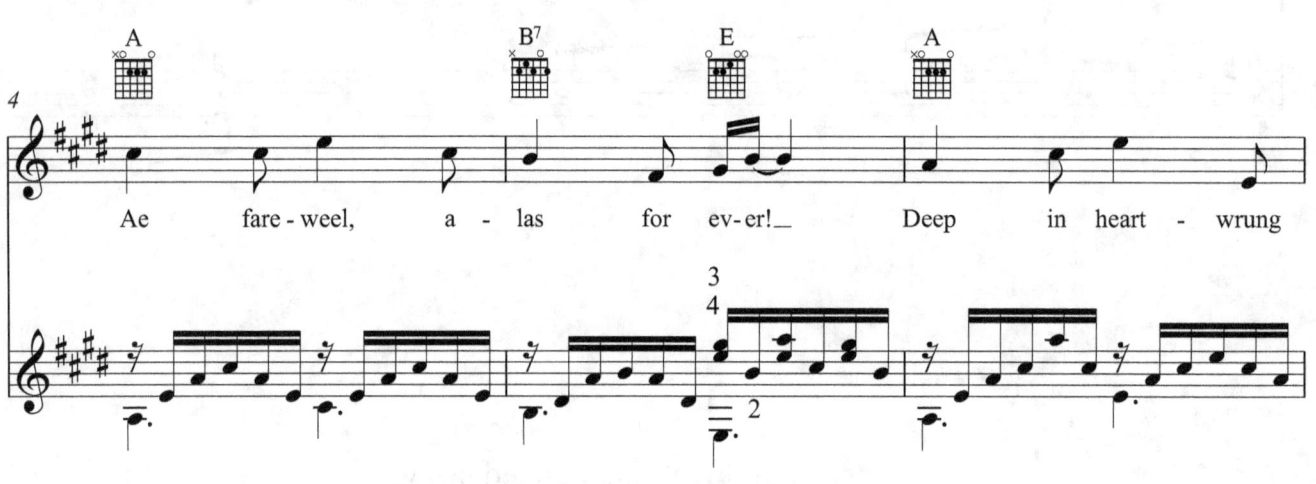

Ae fare - weel, a - las for ev- er!_ Deep in heart - wrung

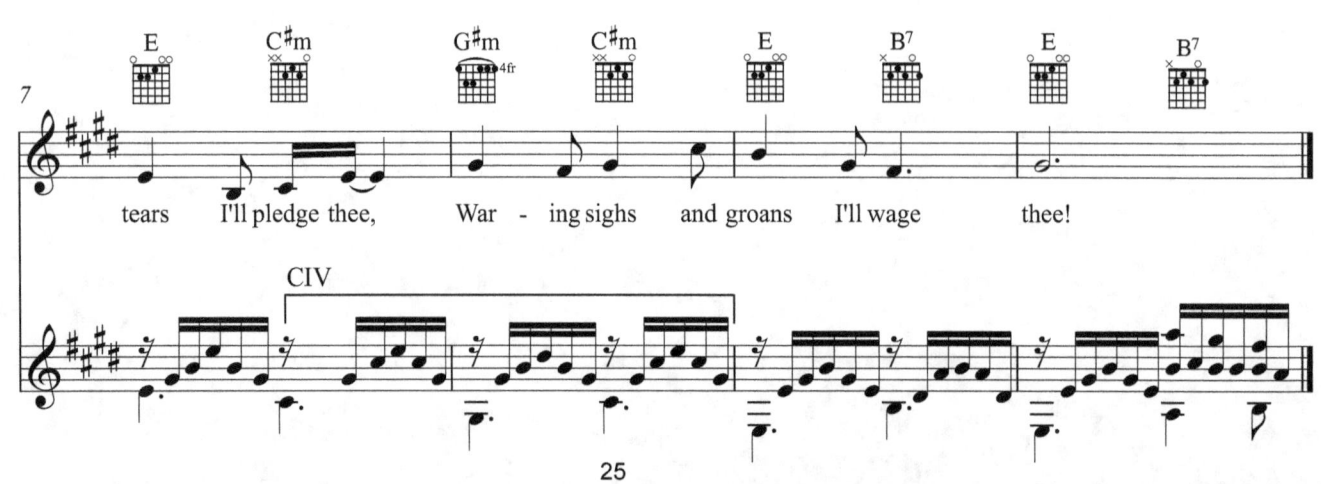

tears I'll pledge thee, War - ing sighs and groans I'll wage thee!

Who shall say that Fortune grieves him
While the star of hope she leaves him?
Me, nae cheerfu' twinkle lights me,
Dark despair around benights me.

I'll ne'er blame my partial fancy,
Naething could resist my Nancy,
For to see her was to love her,
Love but her, and love for ever.

Had we never loved sae kindly,
Had we never loved sae blindly,
Never met—or never parted,
We had ne'er been broken-hearted.

Fare thee weel, thou first and fairest!
Fare thee weel, thou best and dearest!
Thine be ilka joy and treasure,
Peace, enjoyment, love, and pleasure!

Ae fond kiss, and then we sever!
Ae fareweel, alas, for ever!
Deep in heart-wrung tears I'll pledge thee,
Warring sighs and groans I'll wage thee!

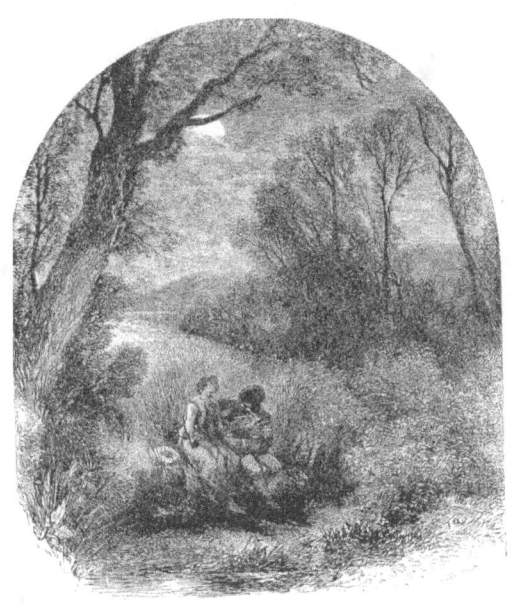

The Soldier's Return

Robert Burns

Traditional

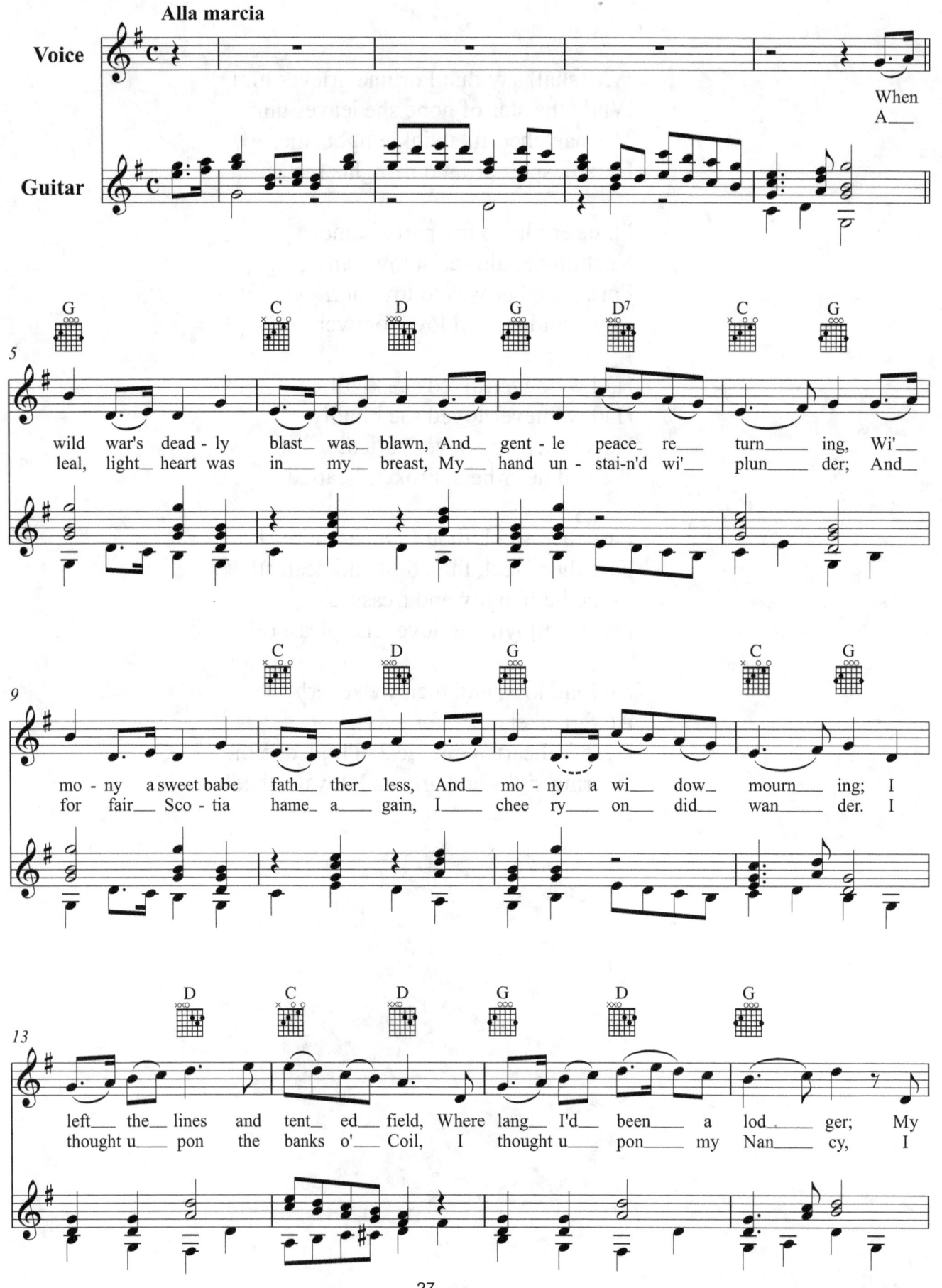

27

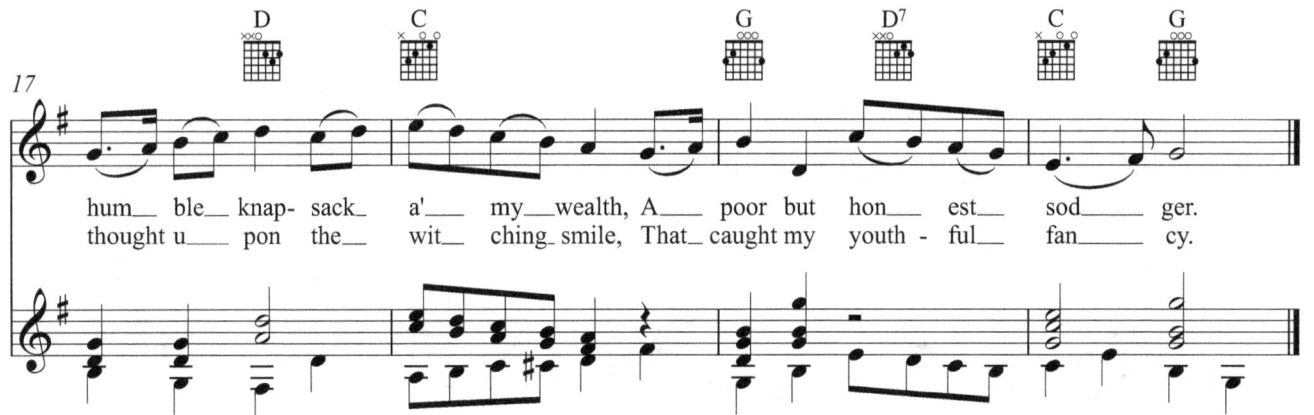

hum_ ble_ knap- sack_ a'_ my_wealth, A_ poor but hon_ est_ sod_____ ger.
thought u_ pon the_ wit_ ching_ smile, That_ caught my youth - ful_ fan____ cy.

3. At length I reach'd the bonnie glen,
Where early life I sported;
I pass'd the mill, and trysting thorn,
Where Nancy aft I courted;
Wha spied I but my ain dear maid,
Down by her mother's dwelling!
And turn'd me round to hide the flood
That in my een was swelling.

4. Wi' alter'd voice, quoth I, Sweet lass,
Sweet as yon hawthorn blossom,
O! happy, happy may he be,
That's dearest to thy bosom!
My purse is light, I've far to gang,
And fain wad be thy lodger;
I've serv'd my king and country lang;
Take pity on a sodger!

5. Sae wistfully she gaz'd on me,
And lovelier was than ever;
Quo' she, a sodger ance I lo'ed,
Forget him shall I never:
Our humble cot, and hamely fare,
Ye freely shall partake it;
That gallant badge, the dear cockade,
Ye're welcome for the sake o't.

6. She gaz'd, she redden'd like a rose,
Syne pale as onie lily;
She sank within my arms and cried,
Art thou my ain dear Willie?
By Him who made yon sun and sky,
By whom true love's regarded,
I am the man; and thus may still
True lovers be rewarded.

7. The wars are o're, and I'm come hame,
And find thee still true-hearted;
Tho' poor in gear, we're rich in love,
And mair we'se ne'er be parted.
Quo' she, My grandsire left me gowd,
A mailen plenish'd fairly;
And come, my faithful sodger lad,
Thou'rt welcome to it dearly.

8. For gold the merchant ploughs the main,
The farmer ploughs the manor;
But glory is the sodger's prize;
The sodger's wealth is honor:
The brave poor sodger ne'er despise,
Nor count him as a stranger,
Remember he's his country's stay,
In day and hour o' danger.

The Weary Pund O' Tow

Robert Burns

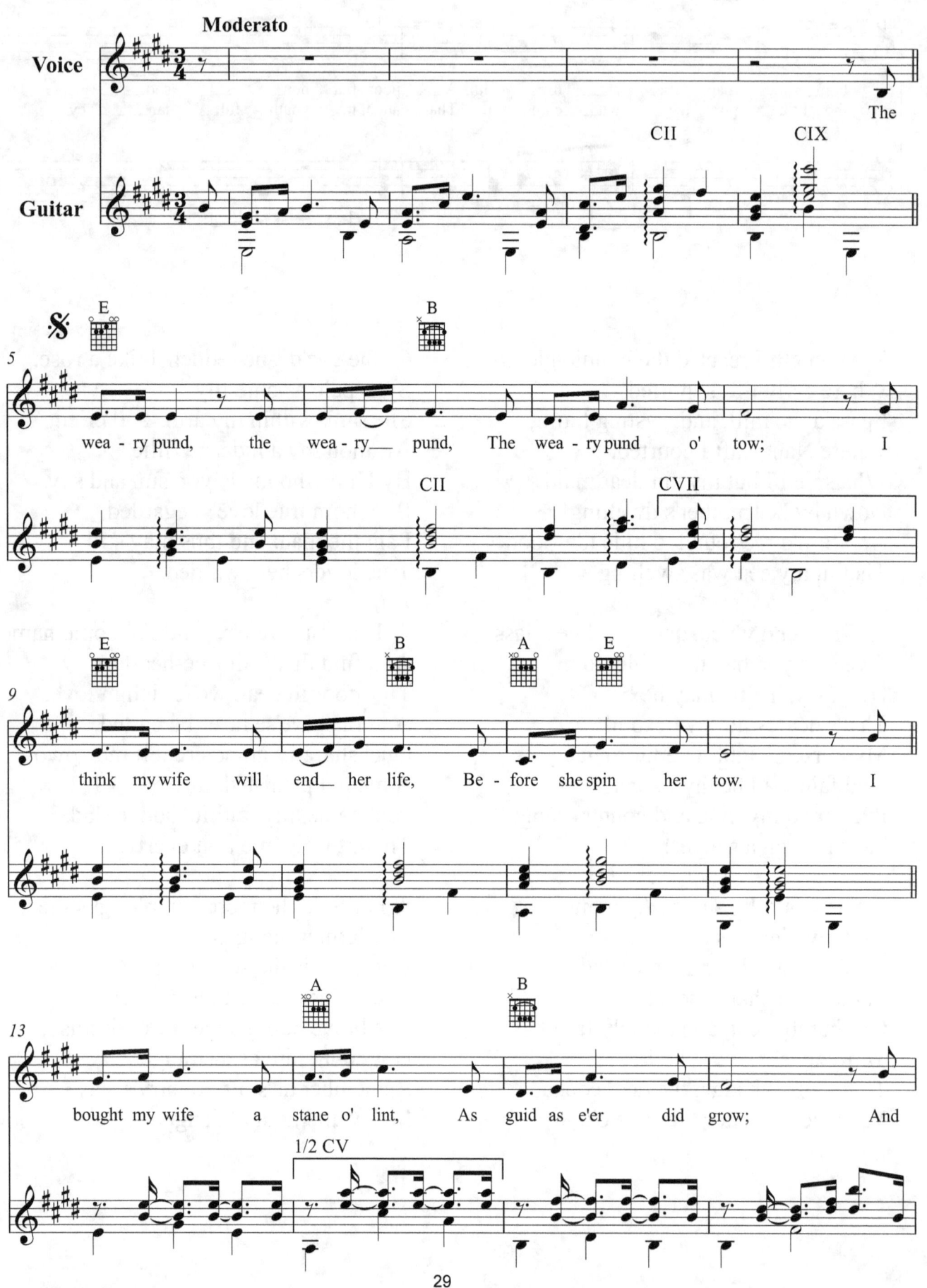

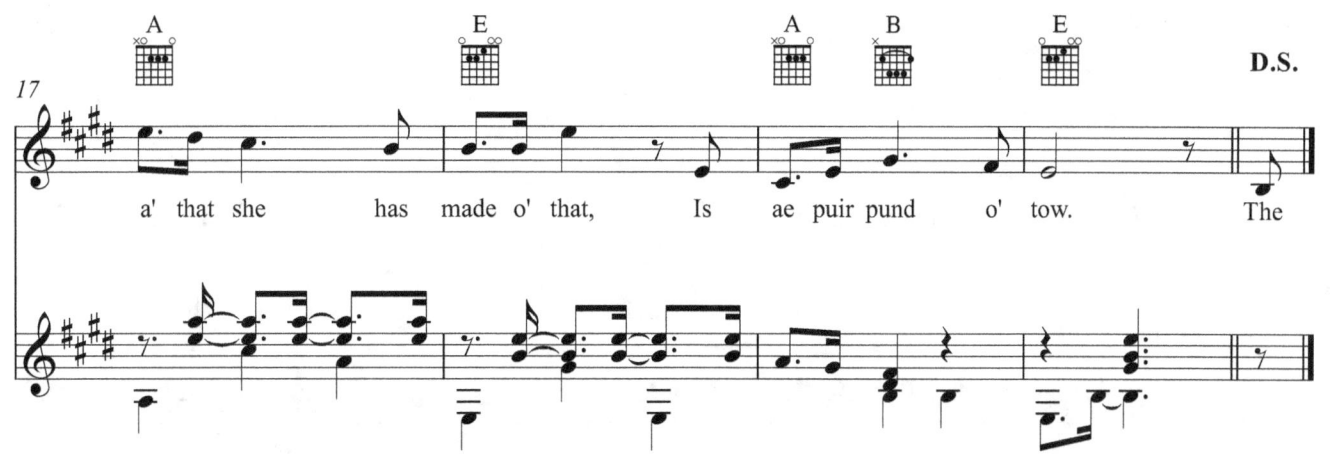

a' that she has made o' that, Is ae puir pund o' tow. The

There sat a bottle in a bole,
A yont the ingle low;
And aye she took the tither souk,
To drouk the stowrie tow.
                    The weary pund etc.

Quoth I, For shame, ye dirty dame,
Gae spin your tap o' tow!
She took the rock, and wi' a knock
She brak it o'er my pow.
                    The weary pund etc.

At last her feet, I sang to see't,
Gaed foremost o'er the knowe;
And or I wad anither jad,
I'll wallop in a tow.
                    The weary pund etc.

My Heart's In The Highlands

Robert Burns

Traditional

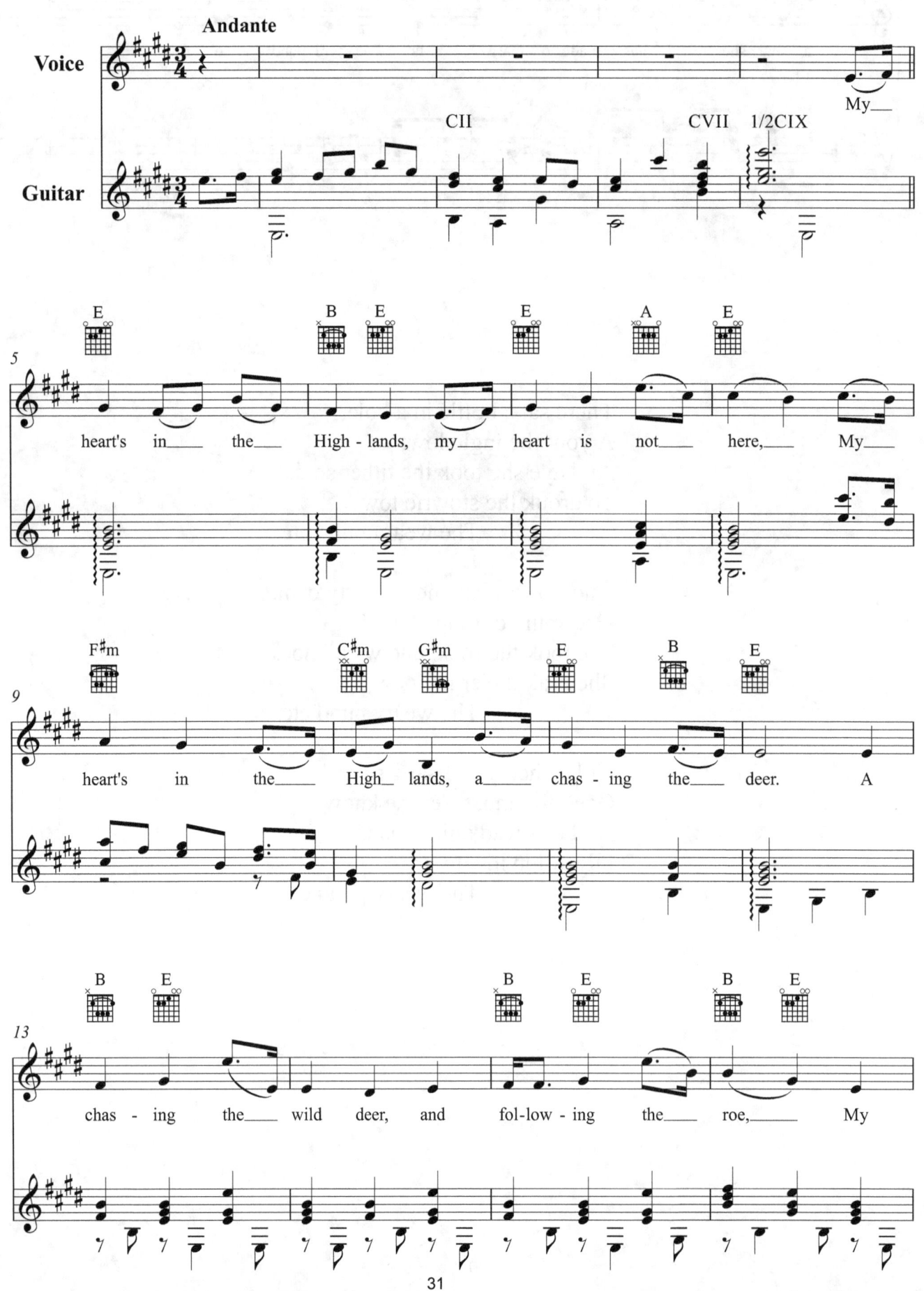

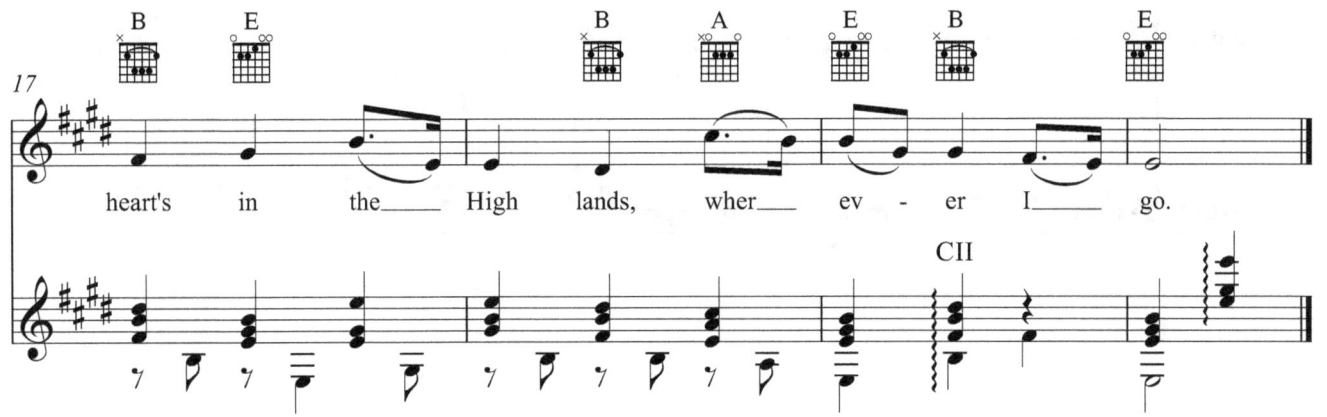

Farewell to the Highlands, farewell to the North,
The birthpace of valour, the country of worth;
Wherever I wander, wherever I rove,
The hills of the Highlands for ever I love.

Farewell to the mountains high cover'd with snow;
Farewell to the straths and green valleys below;
Farewell to the forests and wild-hanging woods;
Farewell to the torrents and loud-pouring floods.

My heart's in the Highlands, my heart is not here,
My heart's in the Highlands a-chasing the deer.
A-chasing the wild deer, and following the roe,
My heart's in the Highlands, wherever I go.

Mary Morison

Robert Burns

Traditional

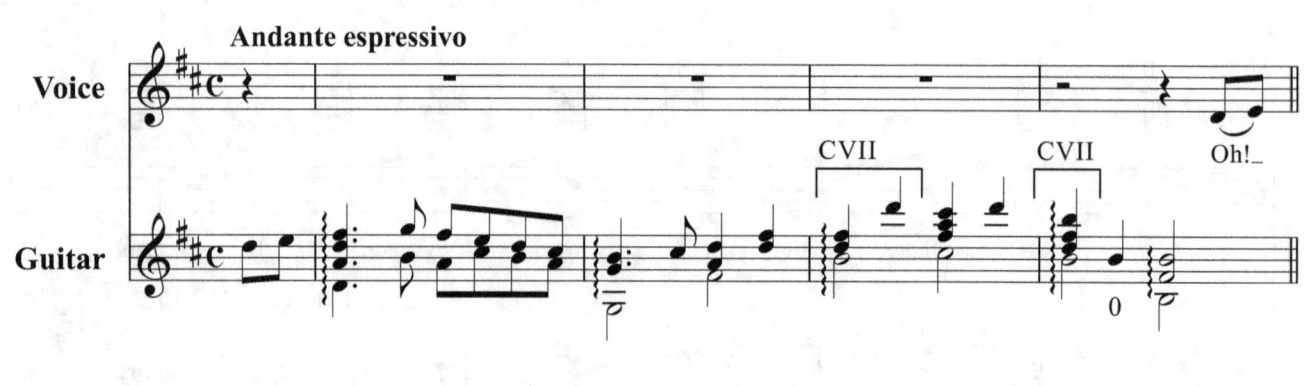

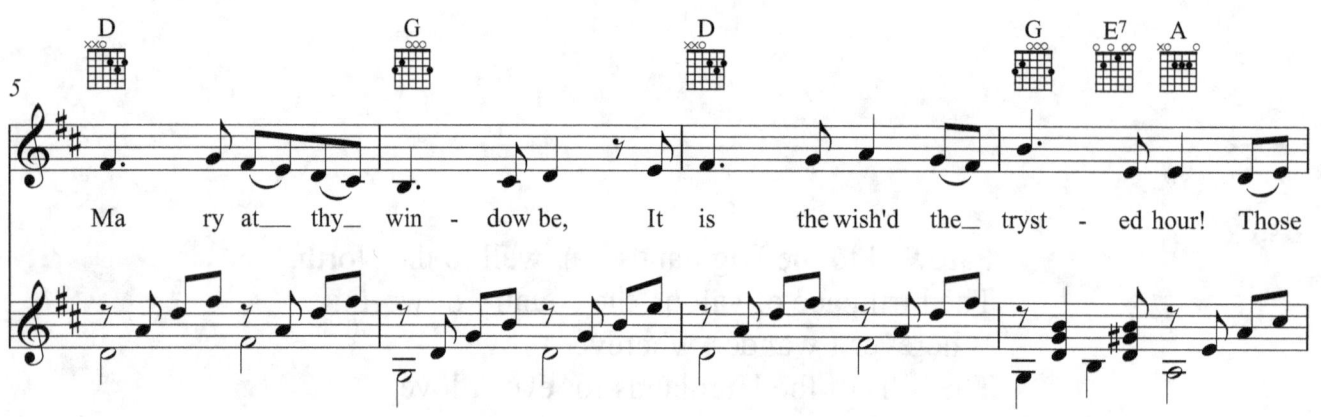

Ma — ry at__ thy__ win - dow be, It is the wish'd the__ tryst - ed hour! Those

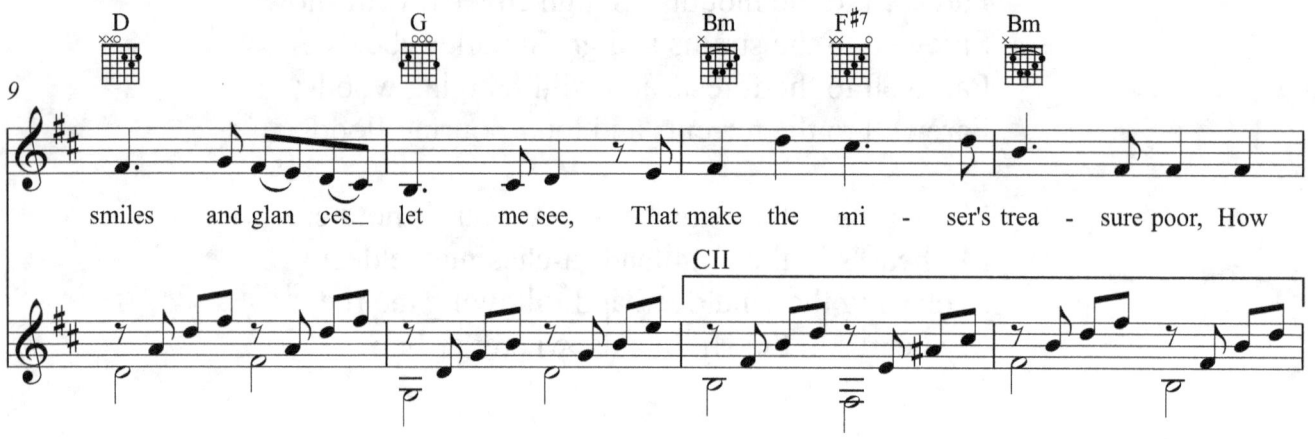

smiles and glan ces__ let me see, That make the mi - ser's trea - sure poor, How

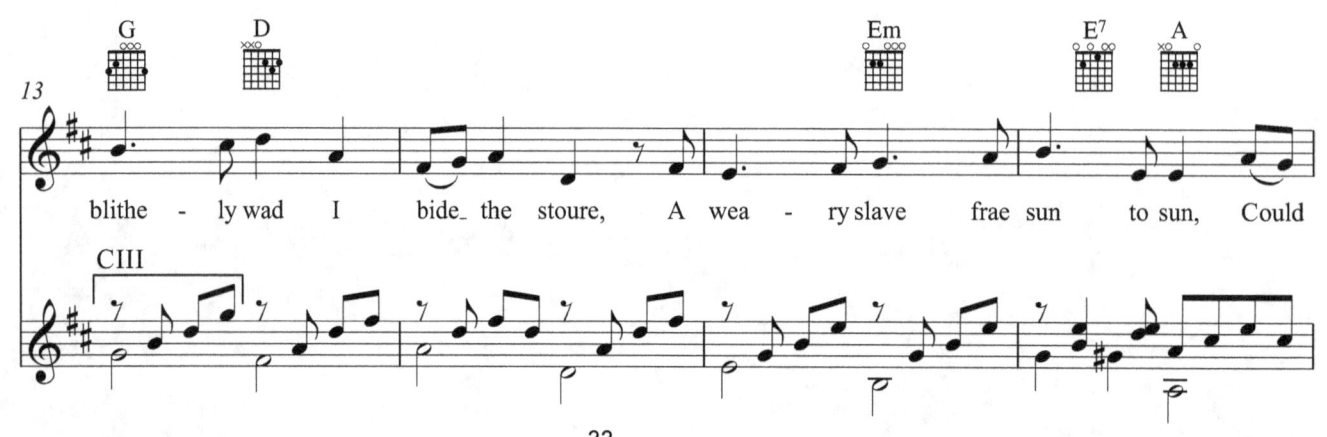

blithe - ly wad I bide__ the stoure, A wea - ry slave frae sun to sun, Could

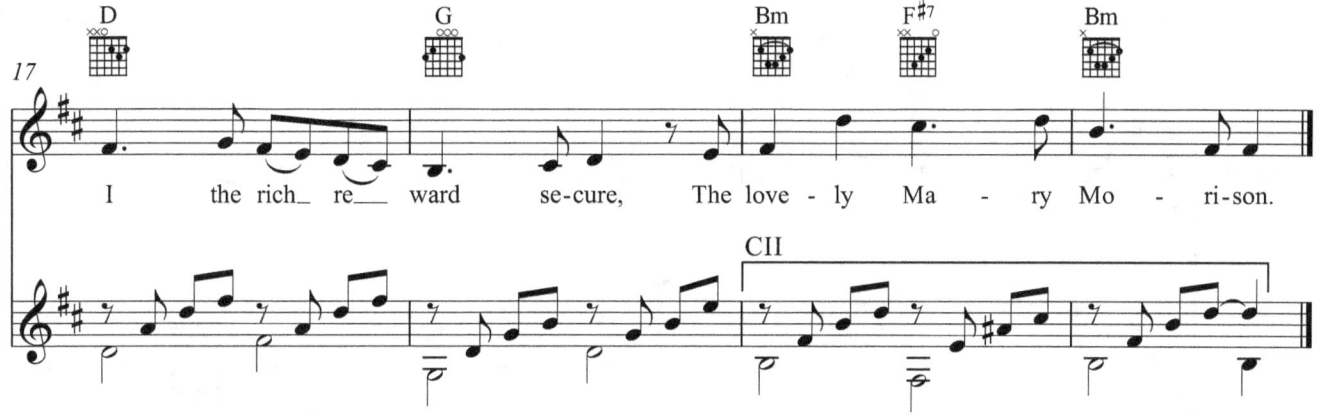

I the rich_ re_ ward se-cure, The love - ly Ma - ry Mo - ri-son.

Yestreen, when to the trembling string
   The dance gaed thro' the lighted ha',
To thee my fancy took its wing,
   I sat, but neither heard, nor saw:
Tho' this was fair, and that was braw,
   And yon the toast of a' the town,
I sigh'd, and said amang them a',
   "Ye are na Mary Morison."

O Mary, canst thou wreck his peace,
   Wha for thy sake wad gladly die?
Or canst thou break that heart of his,
   Whase only fault is loving thee?
If love for love thou wilt na gi'e,
   At least be pity to me shown!
A thought ungentle canna be
   The thought o' Mary Morison.

Ye Banks and Braes

Robert Burns

Traditional

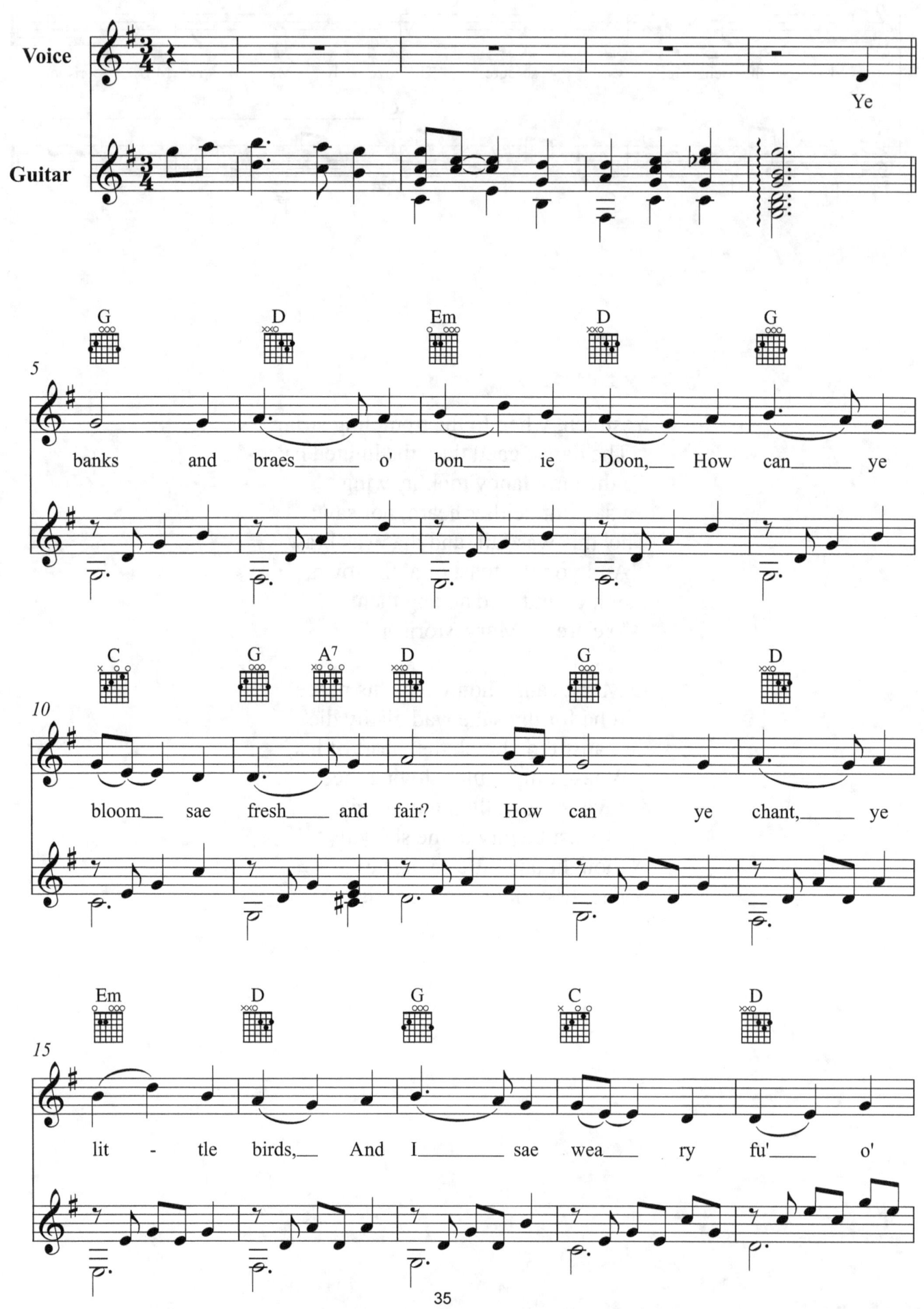

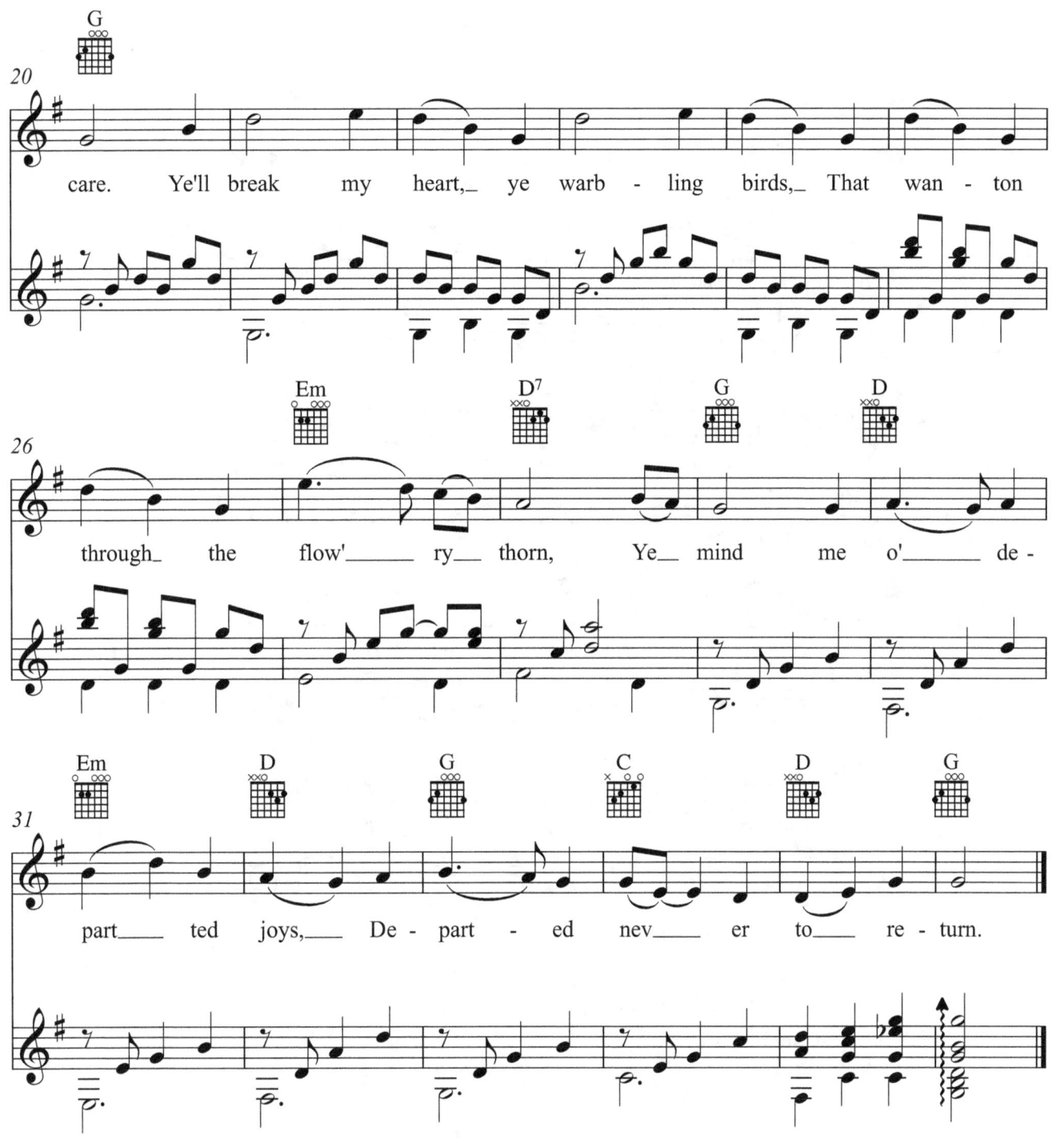

Oft hae I rov'd by bonnie Doon
To see the rose and woodbine twine;
When ilka bird sang o' its love,
And fondly sae did I o' mine.

Wi' lightsome heart I pu'd a rose,
Fu' sweet upon its thorny tree;
But my fause lover stole my rose,
And, ah! he left the thorn wi' me.

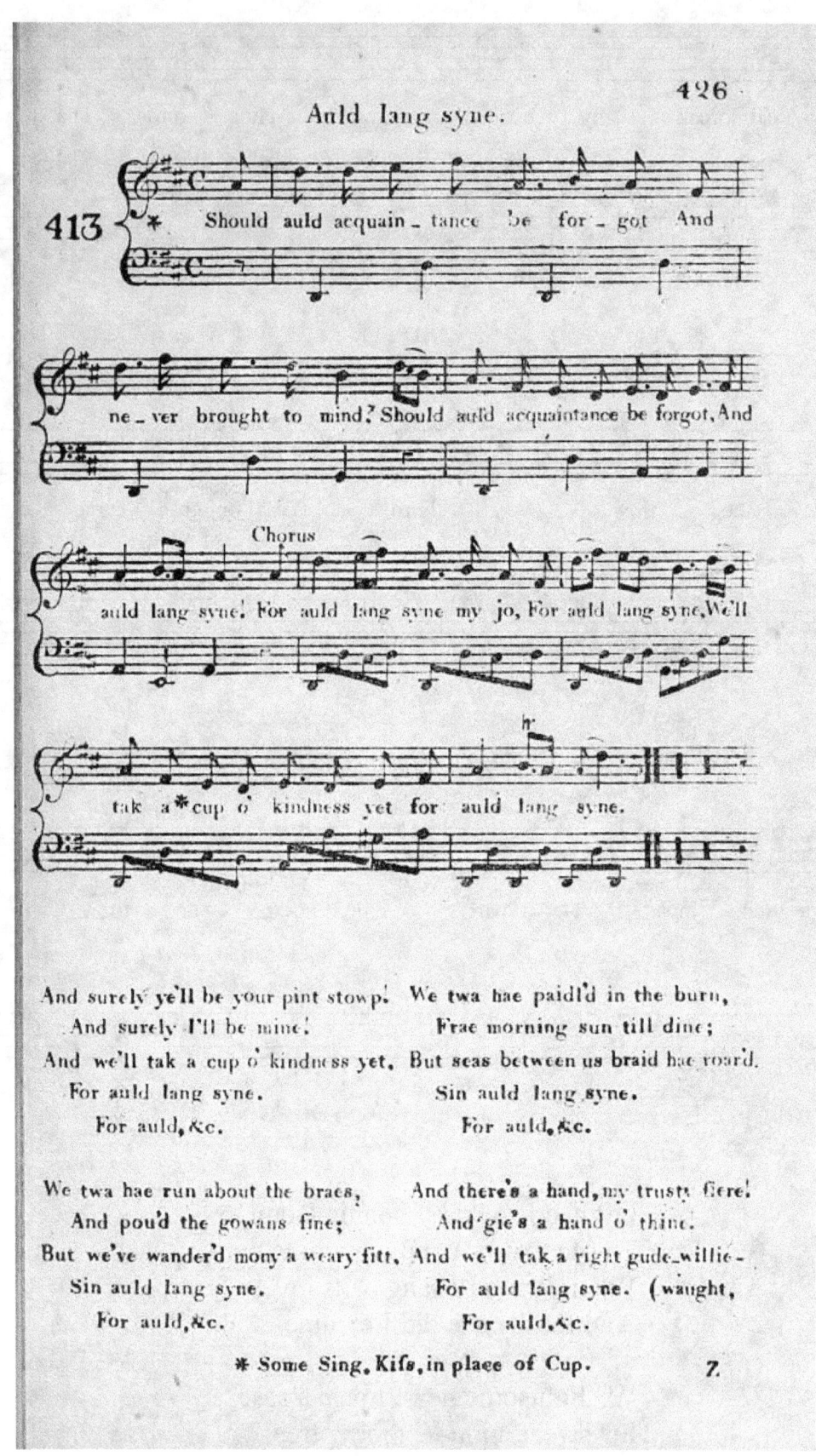

The Original Version of Auld Lang Syne from Scots Musical Museum Vol.5

Appendix 1

Songs Arranged For Guitar

&

Guitar,

Flute or Recorder

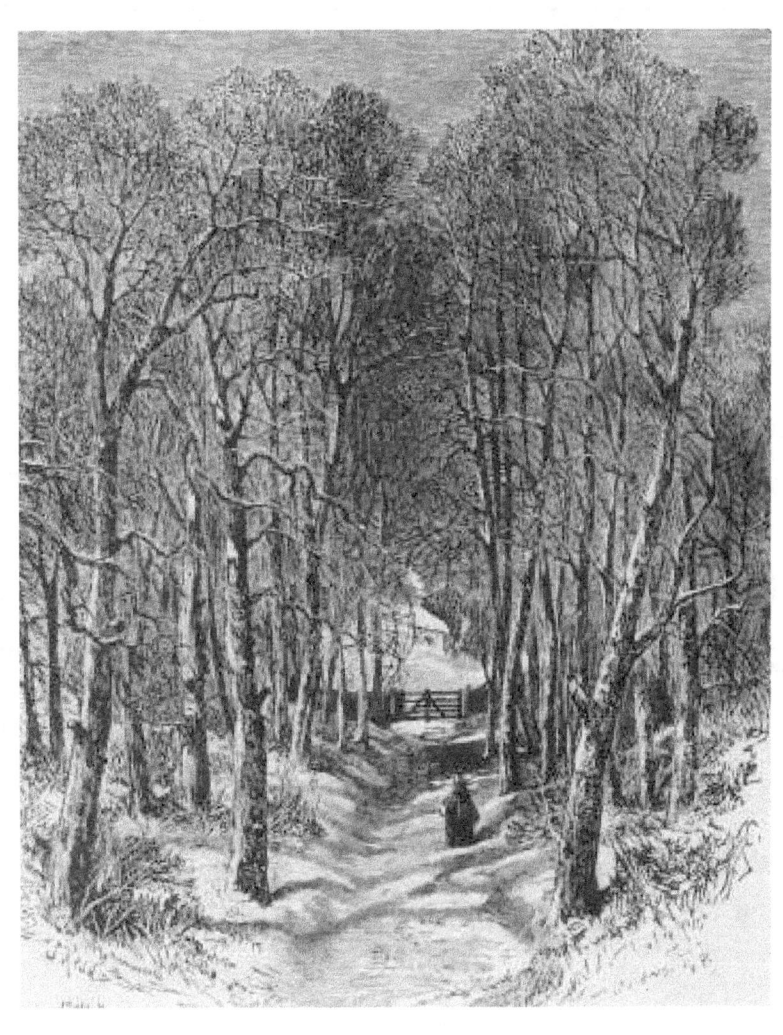

My Love Is Like a Red, Red Rose

Robert Burns

Traditional

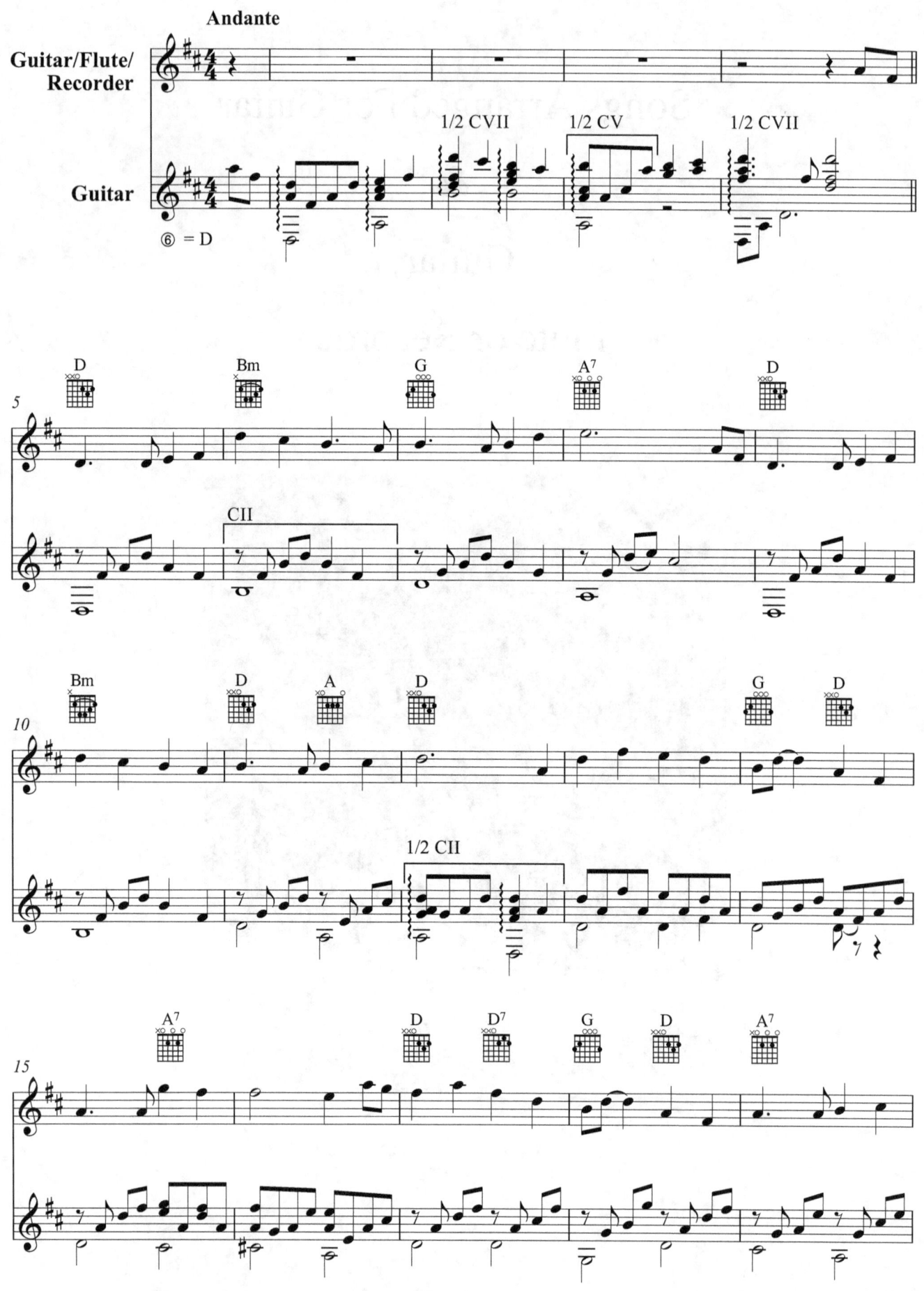

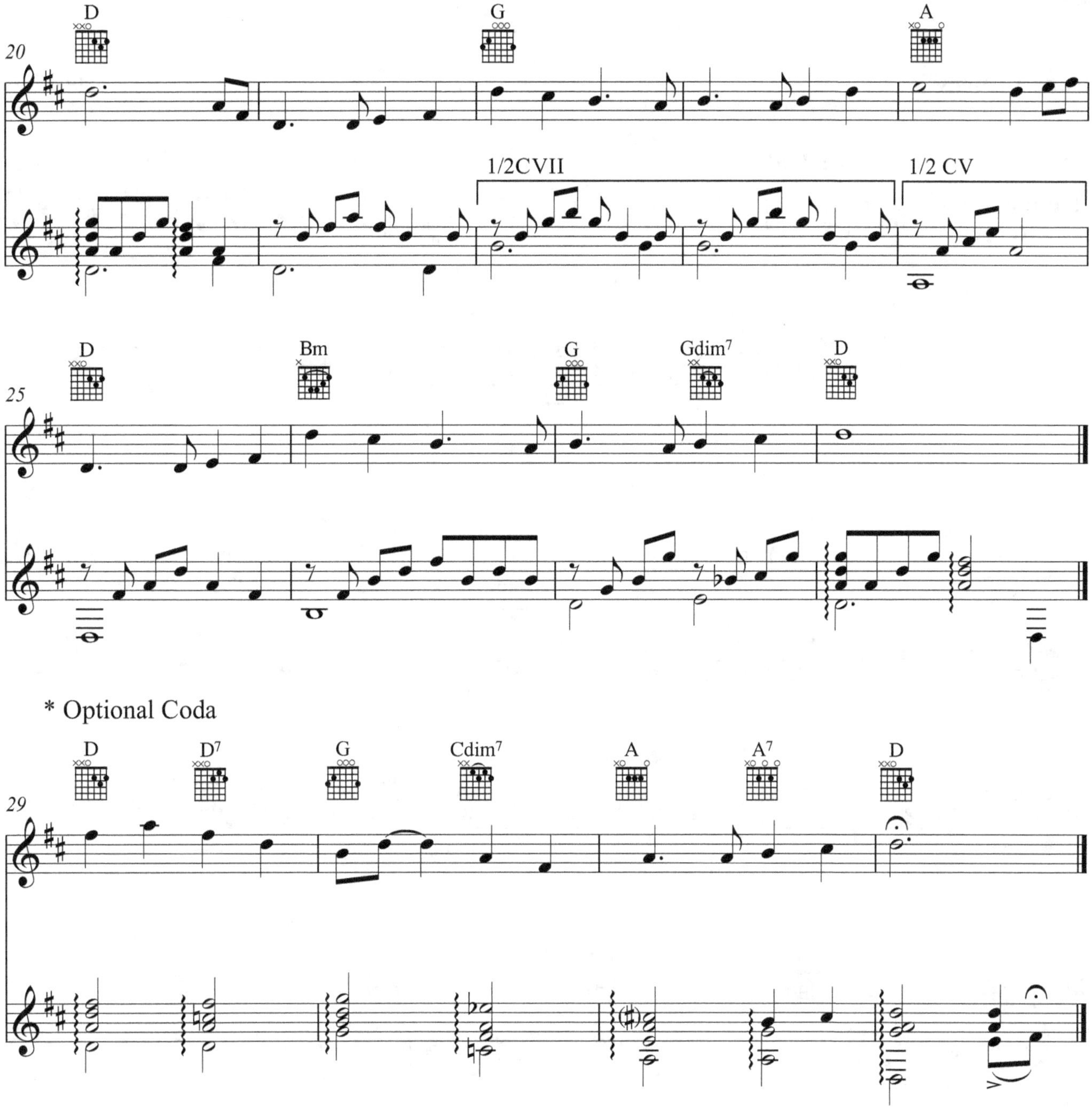

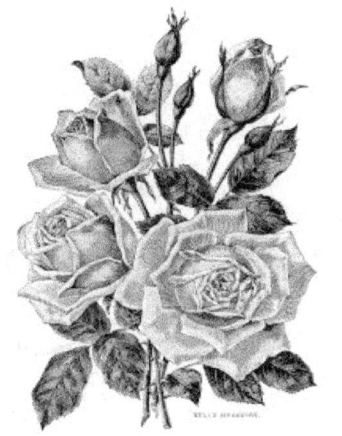

Afton Water (Original Version)

Robert Burns

Traditional

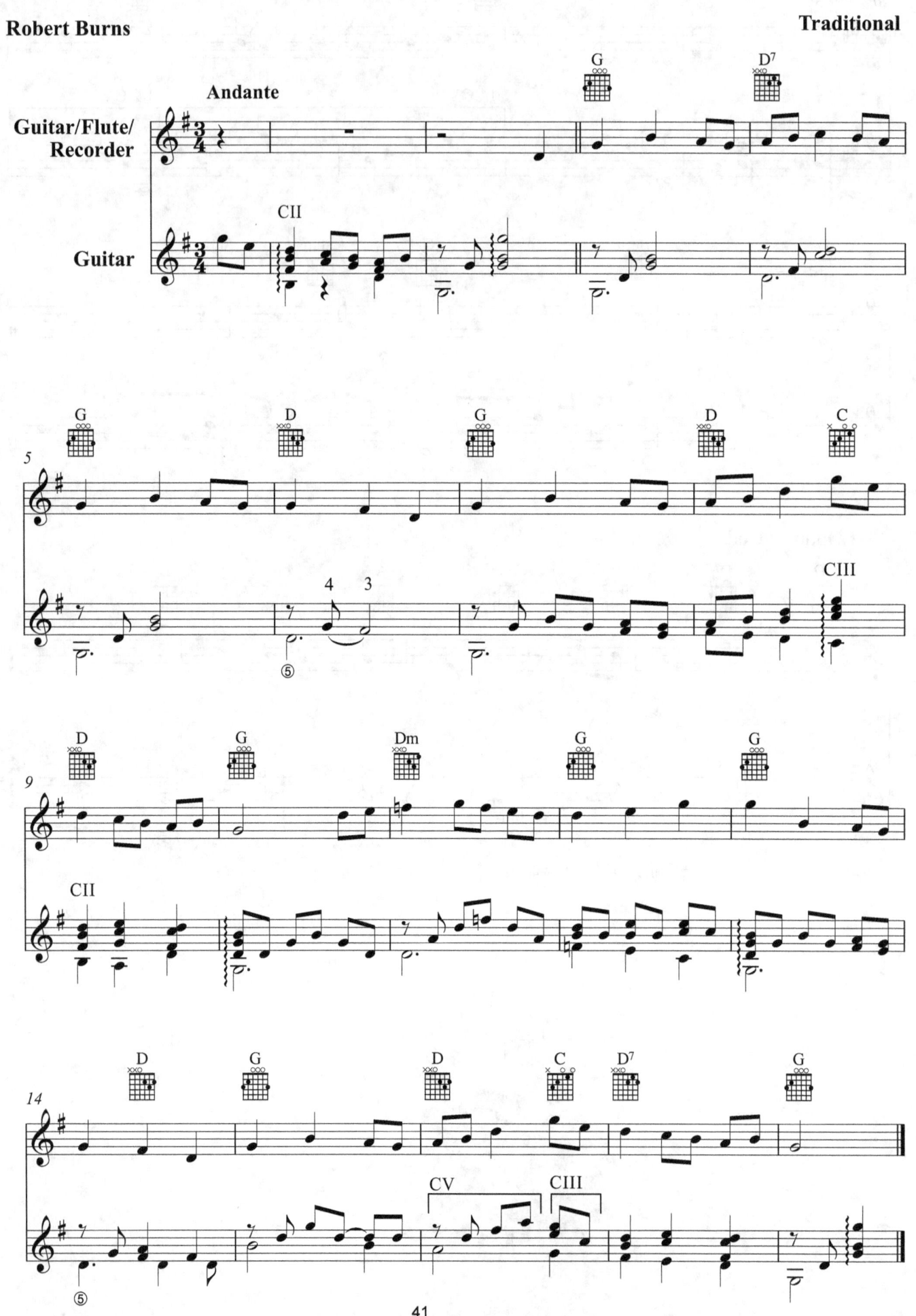

John Anderson, my Jo

Robert Burns

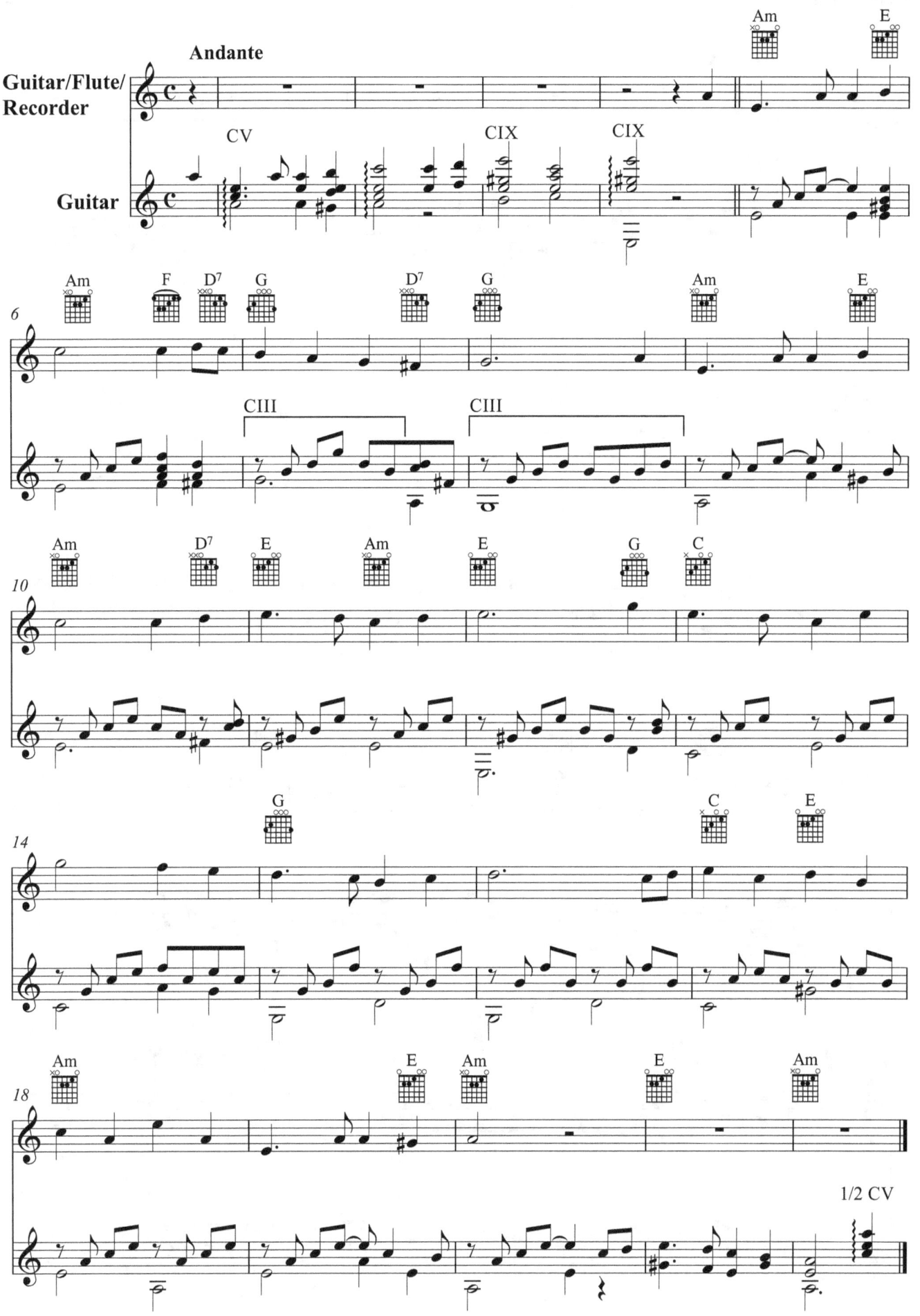

Afton Water

Robert Burns

Alexander Hume

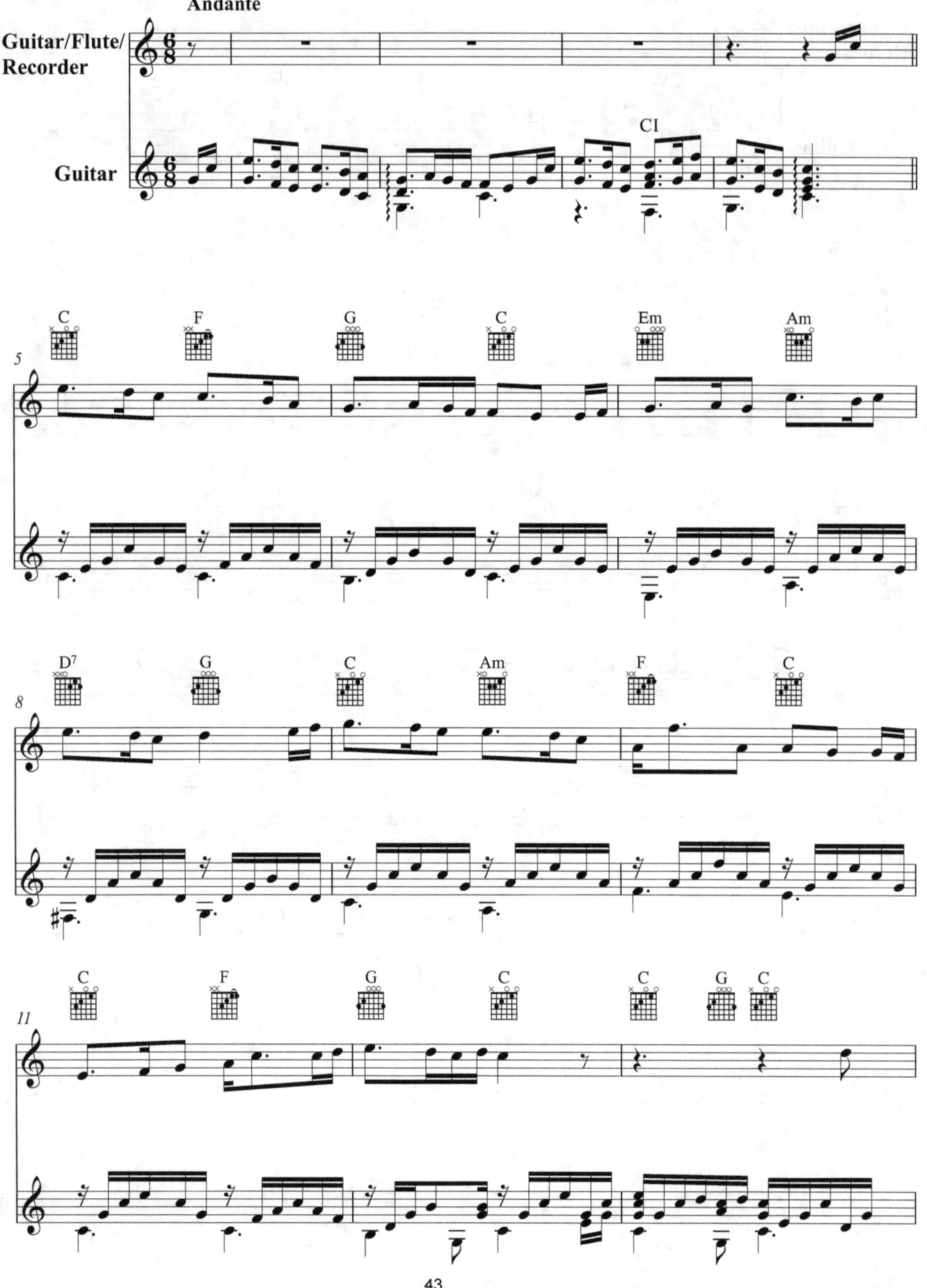

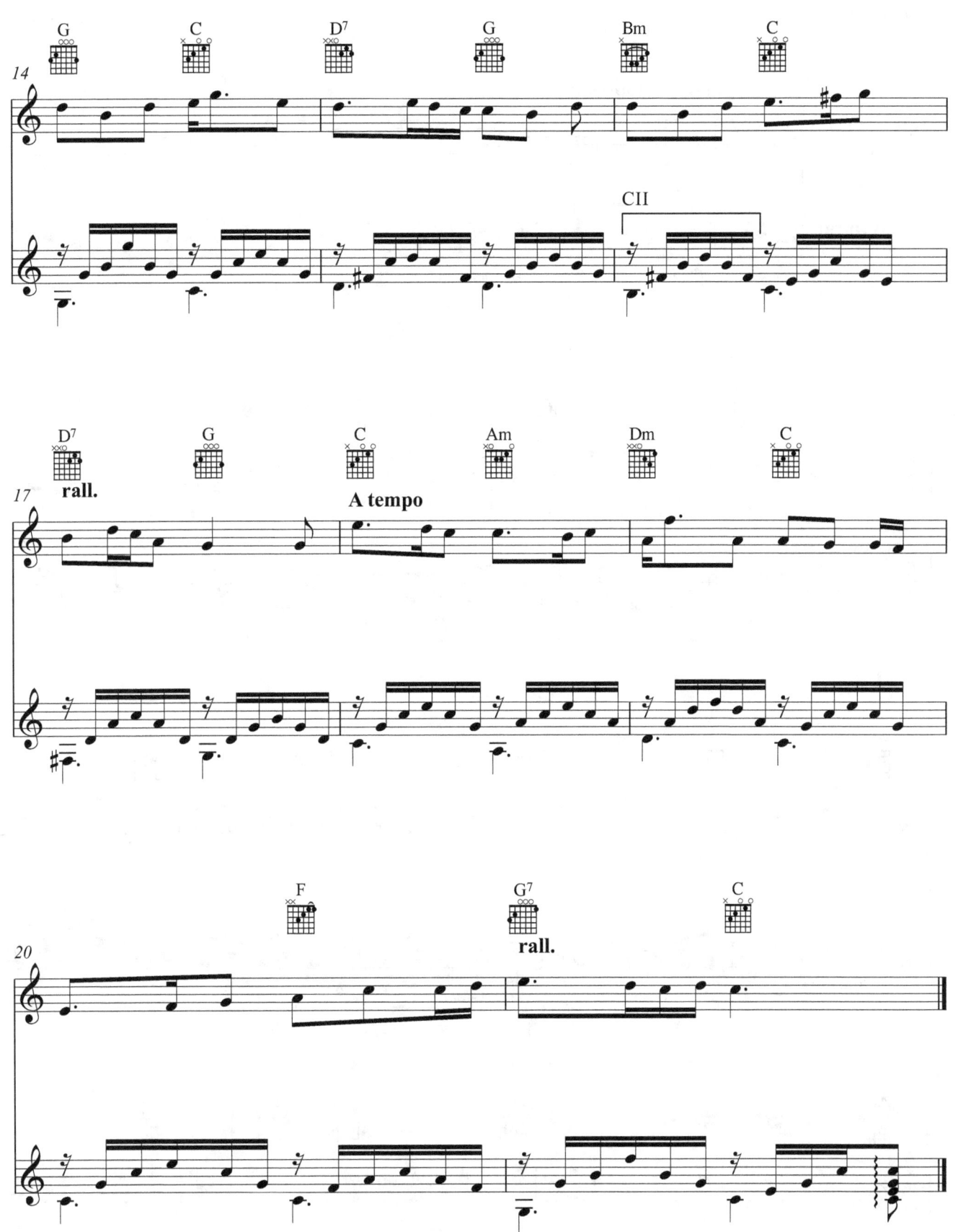

Lord Gregory

Robert Burns

Traditional

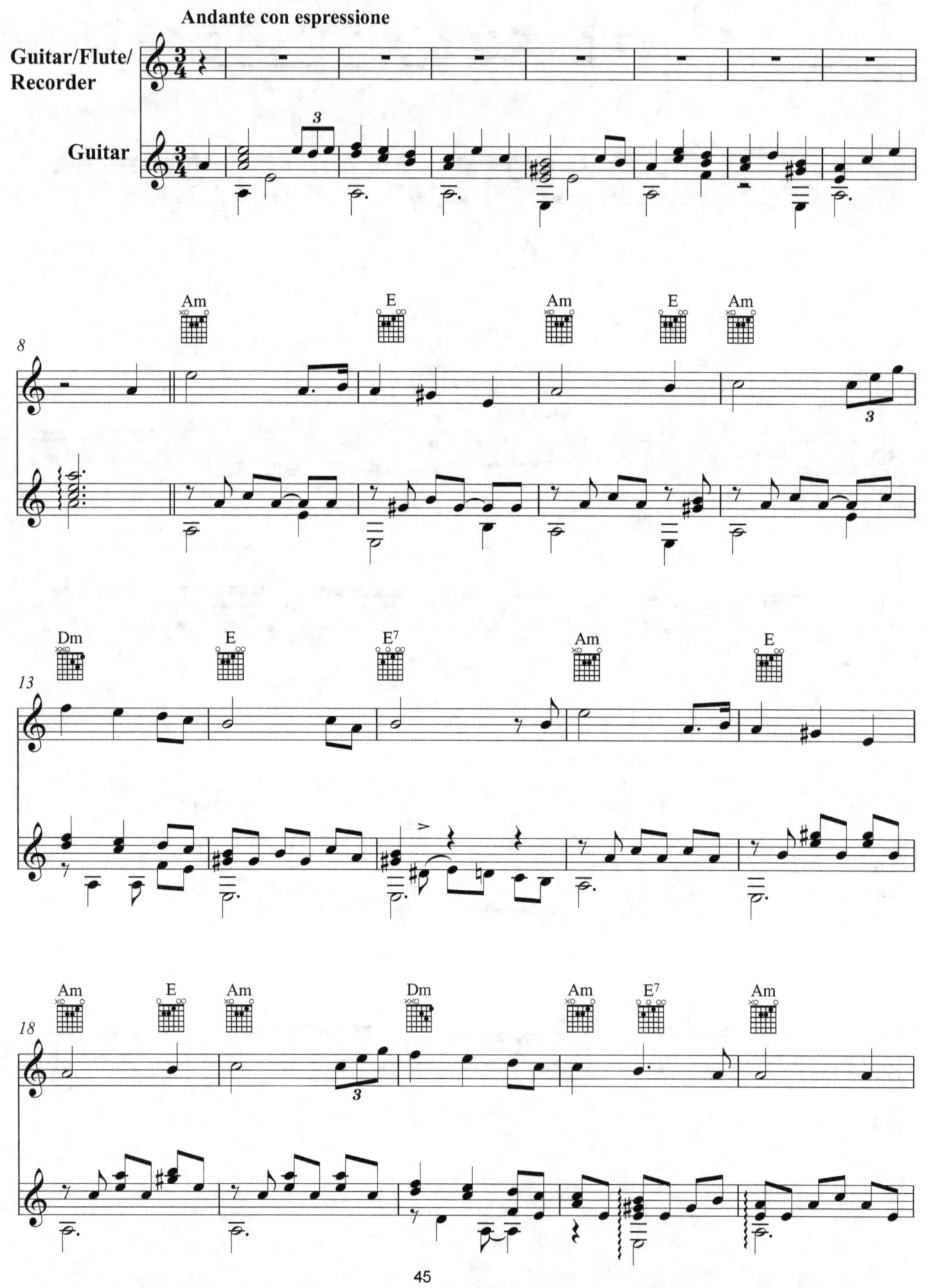

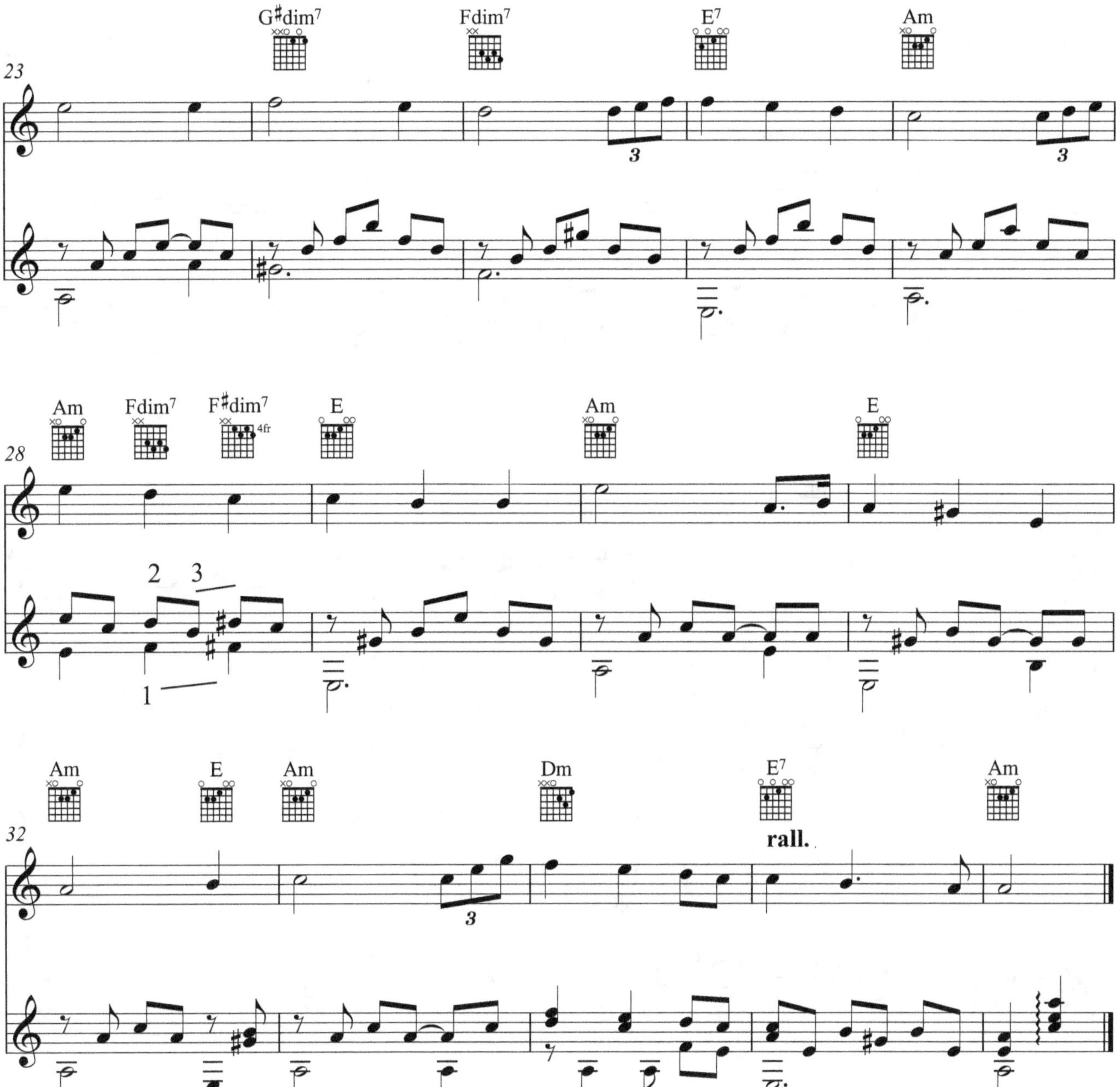

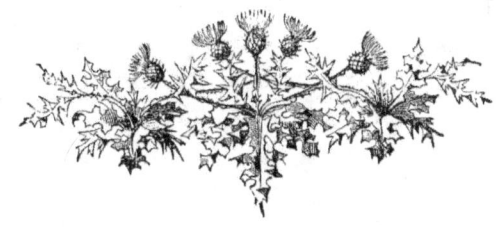

Auld Lang Syne (Original Version)

Robert Burns

Traditional

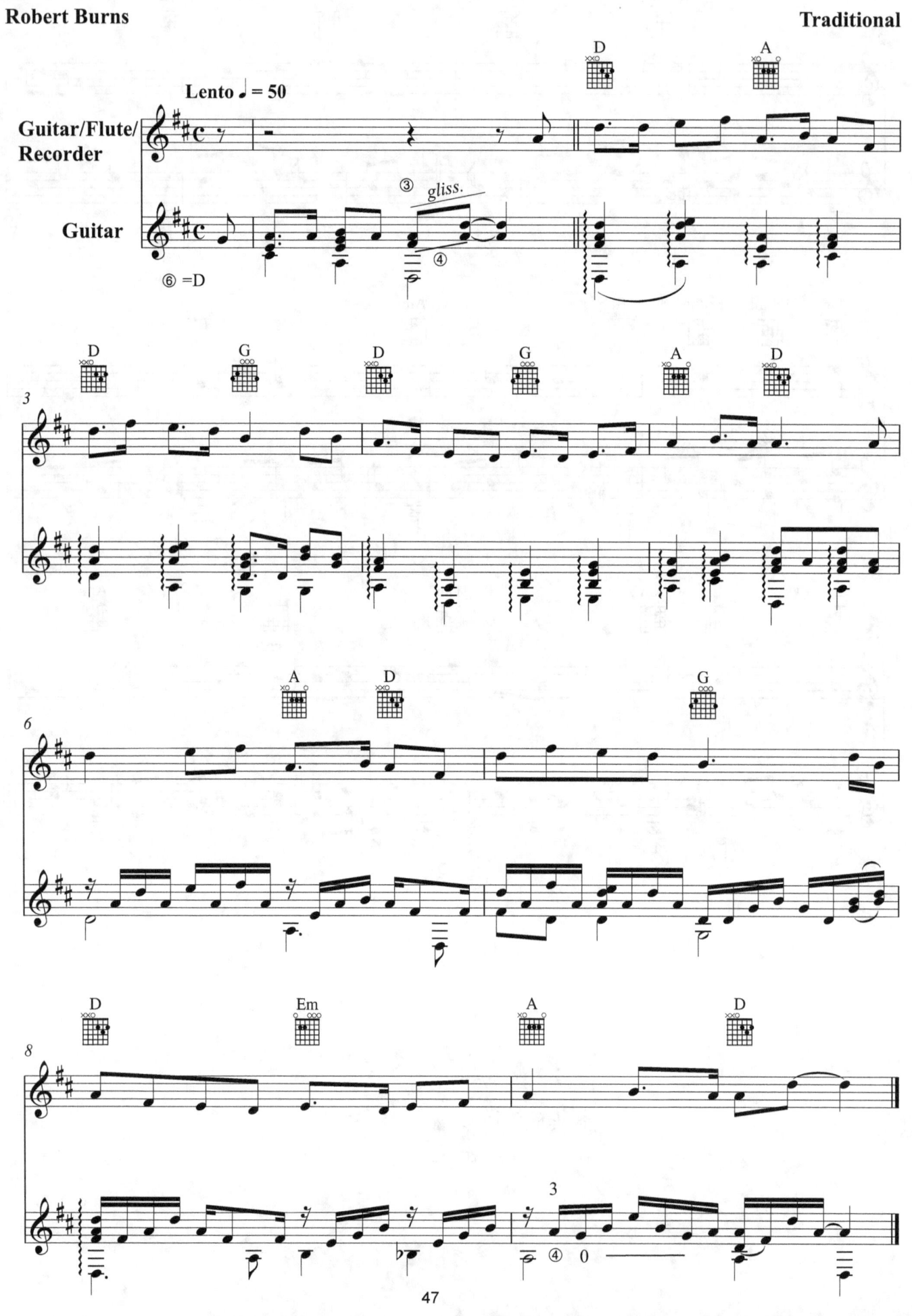

Ae Fond Kiss

Robert Burns

Traditional

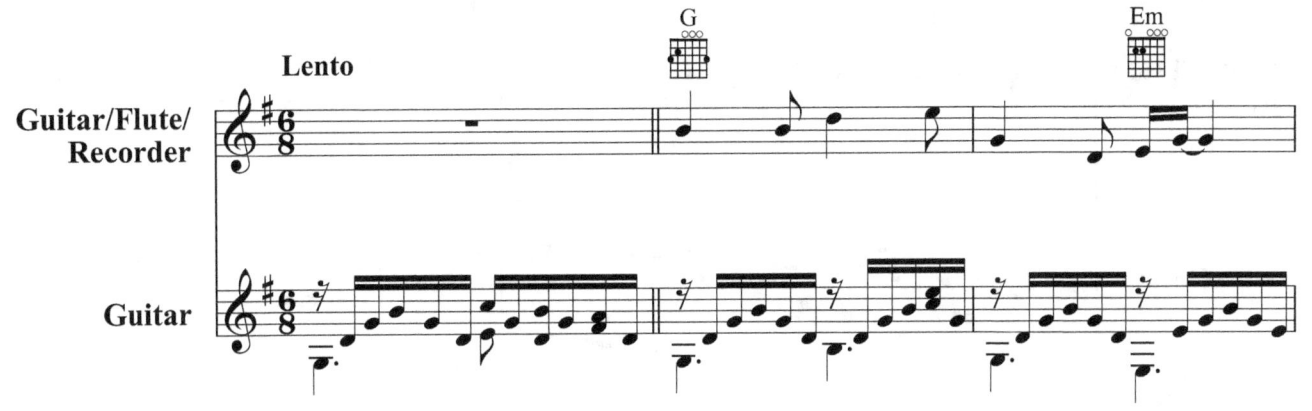

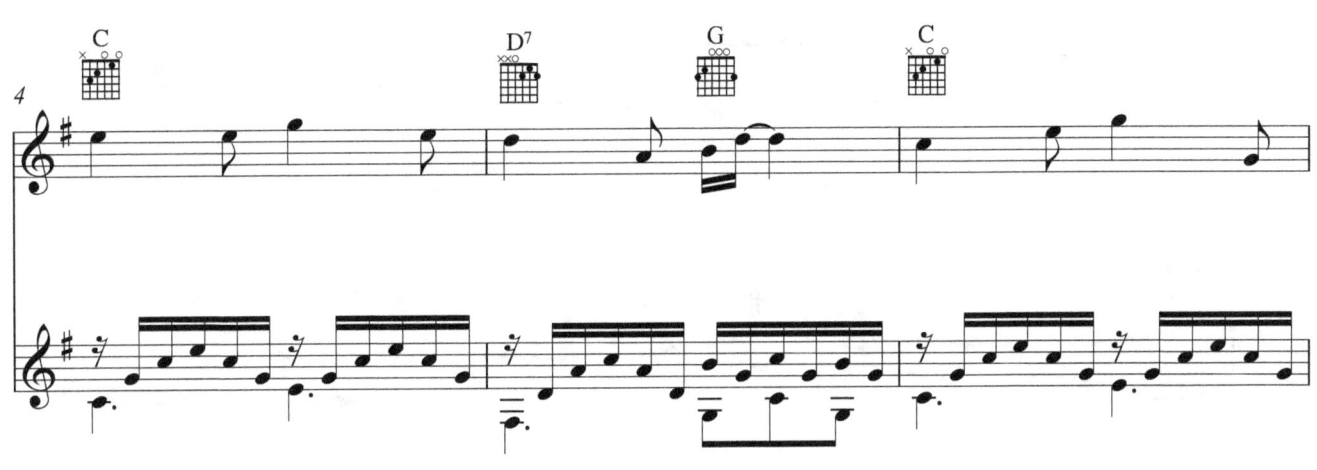

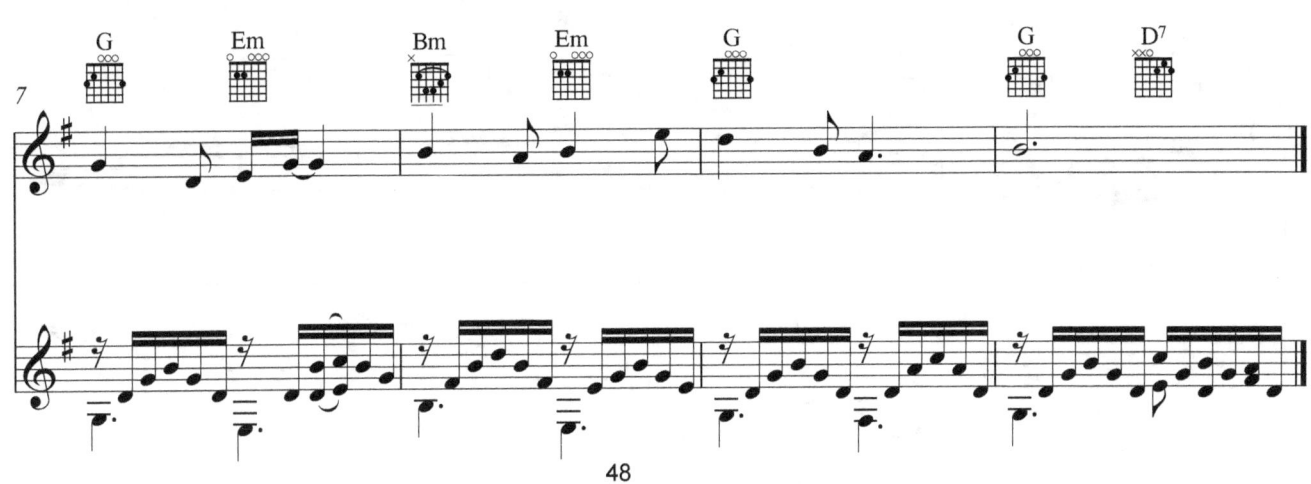

48

My Love She's But A Lassie

Robert Burns

Traditional

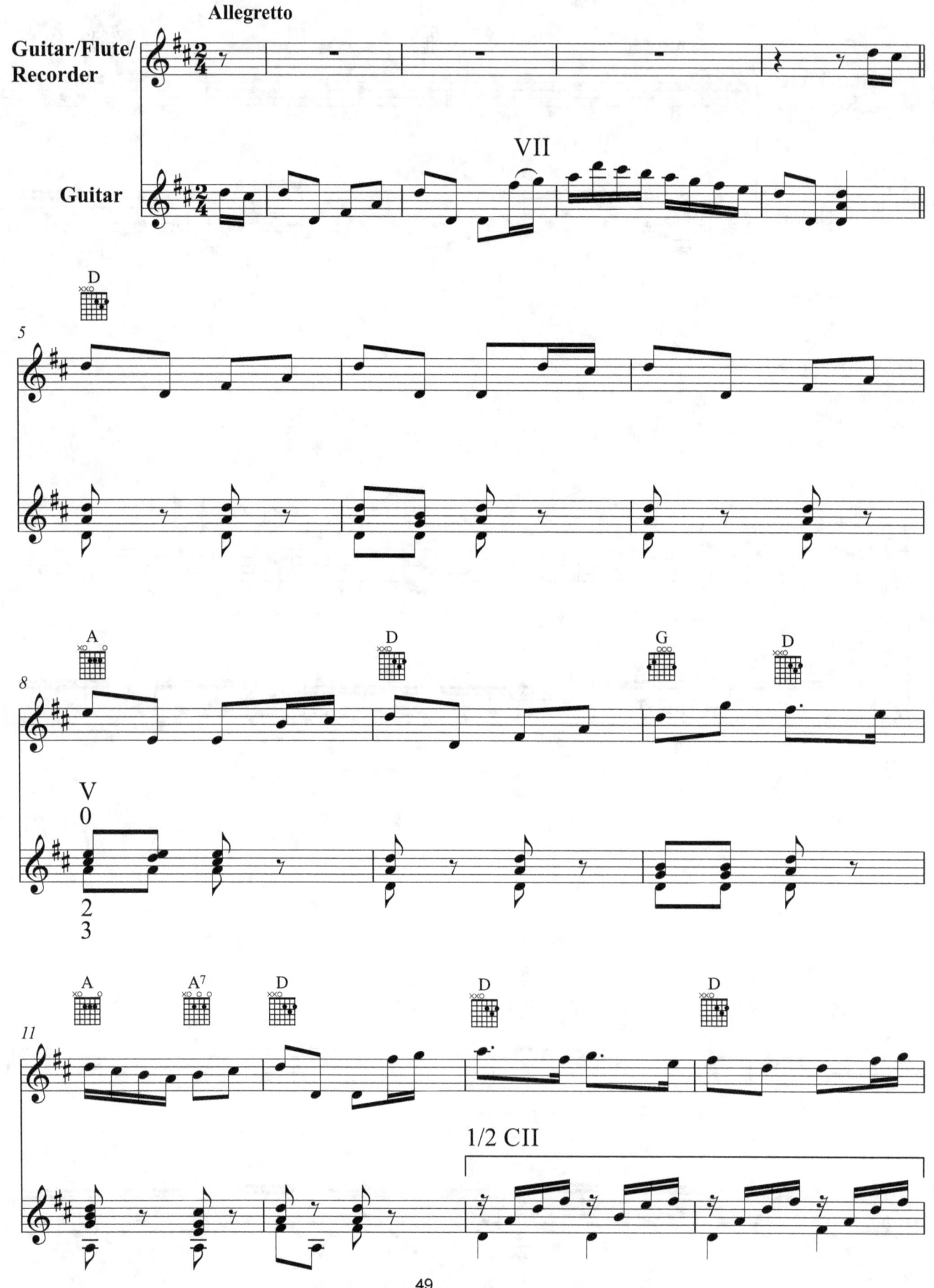

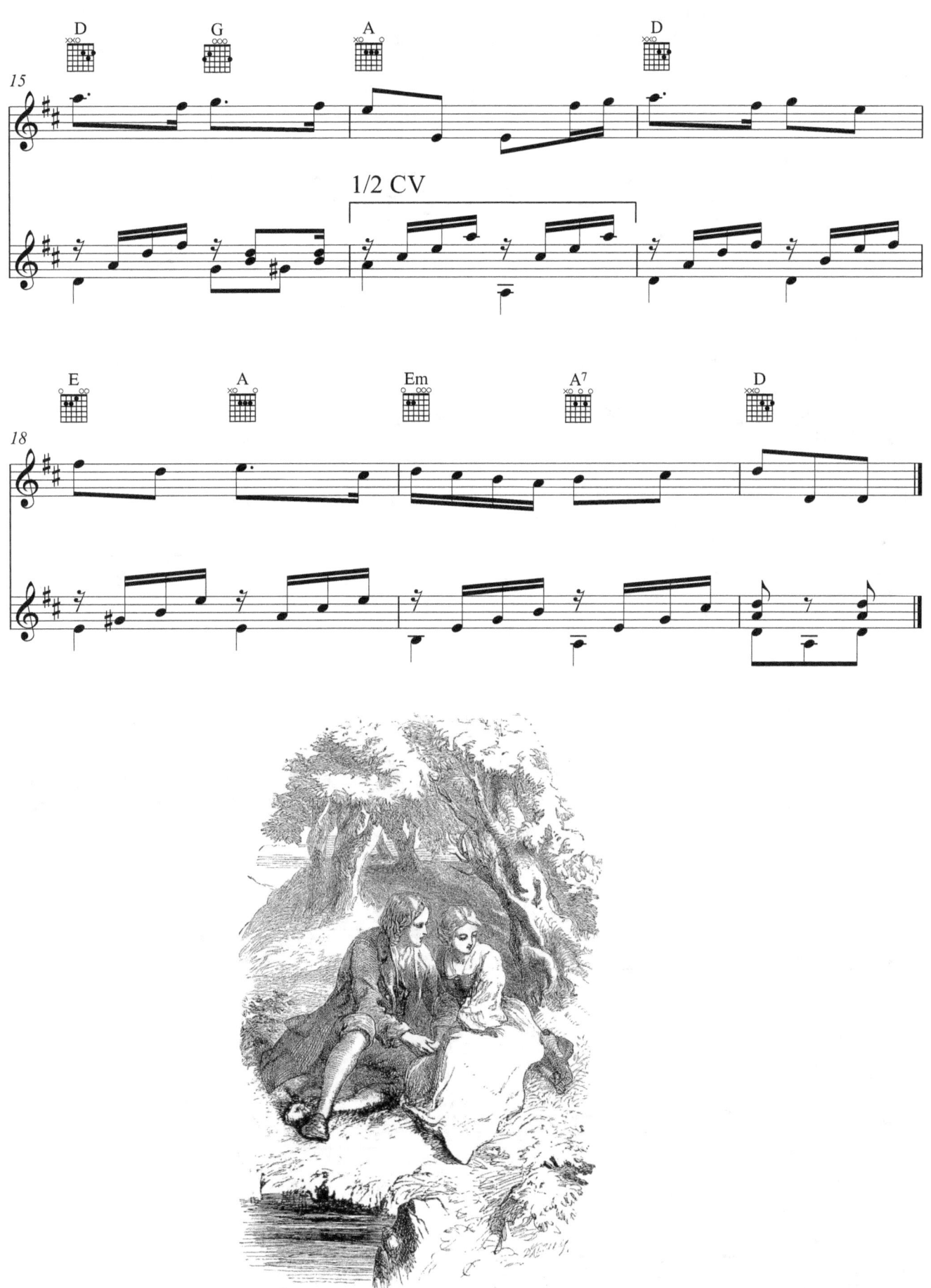

O Lay Thy Loof In Mine, Lass

Robert Burns

Traditional

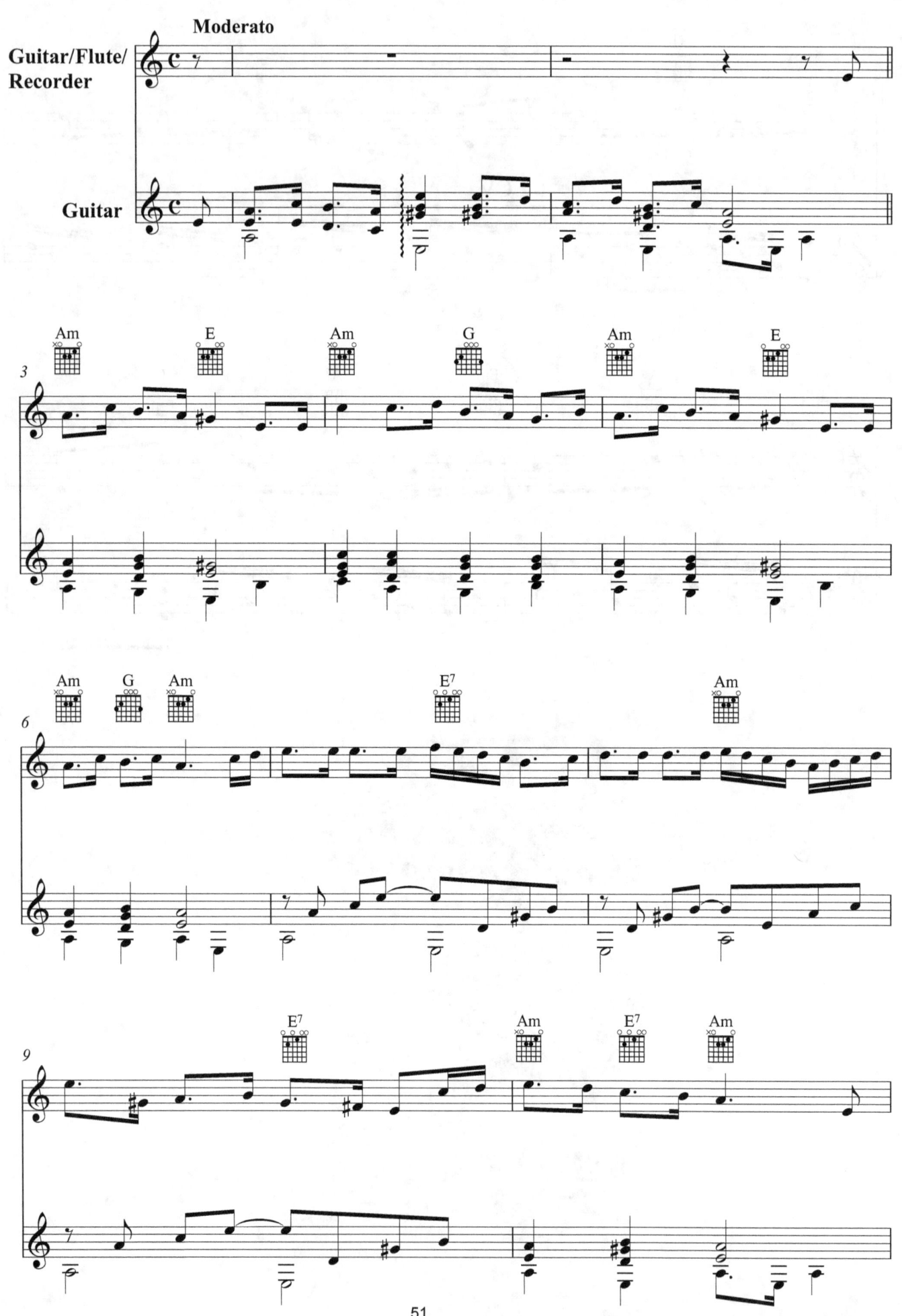

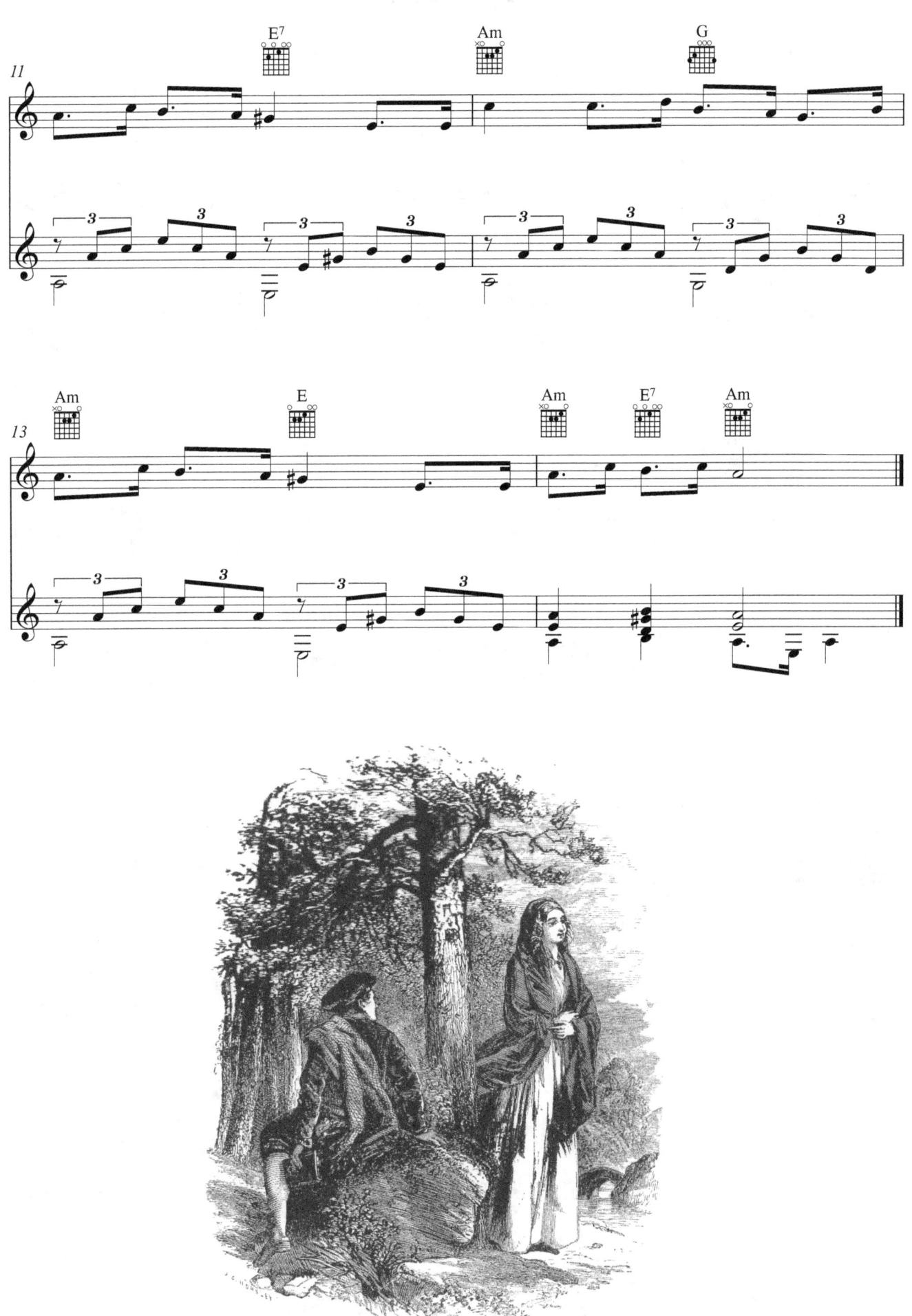

The Weary Pund O' Tow

Robert Burns

Traditional

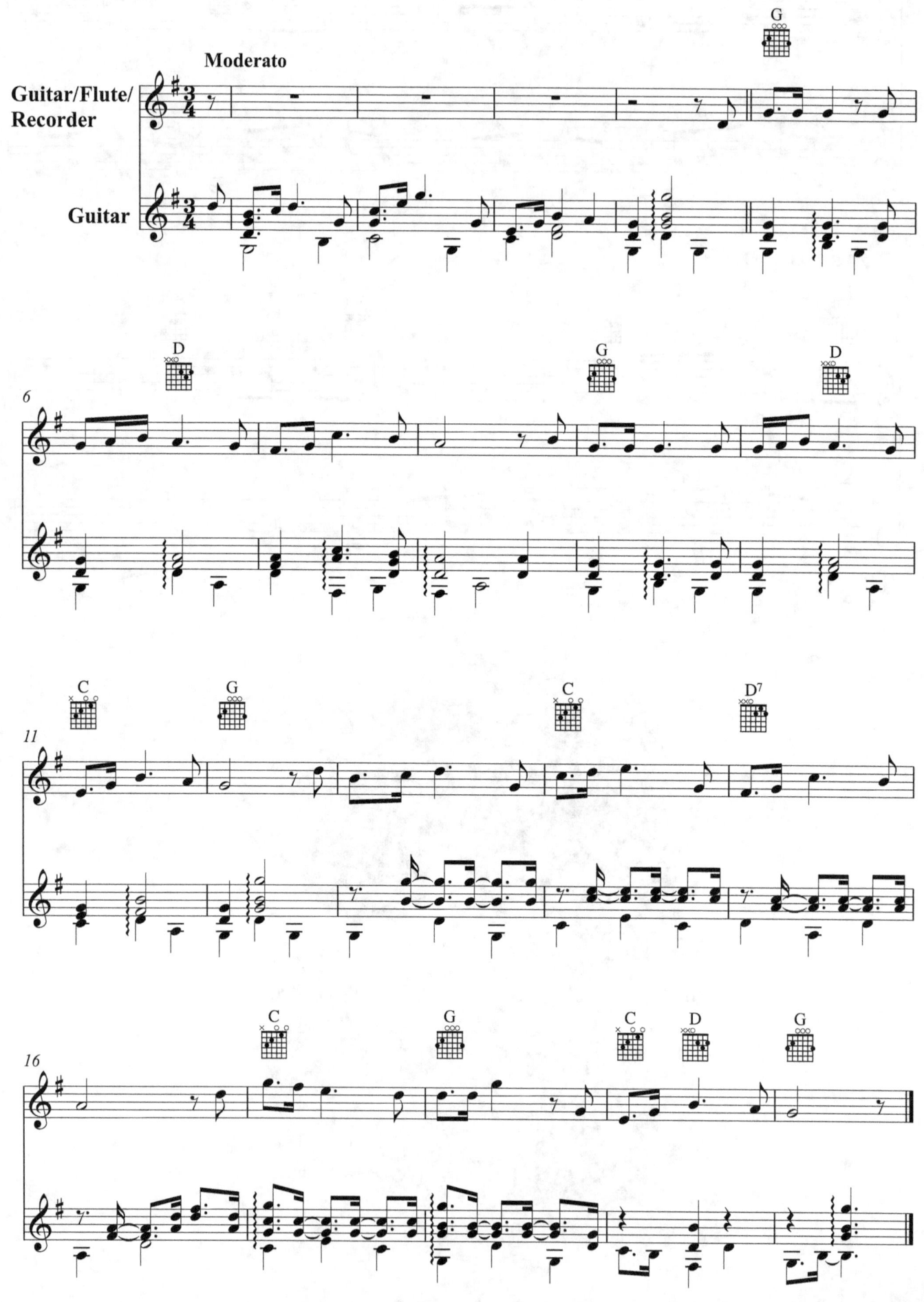

My Heart's In The Highlands

Robert Burns

Traditional

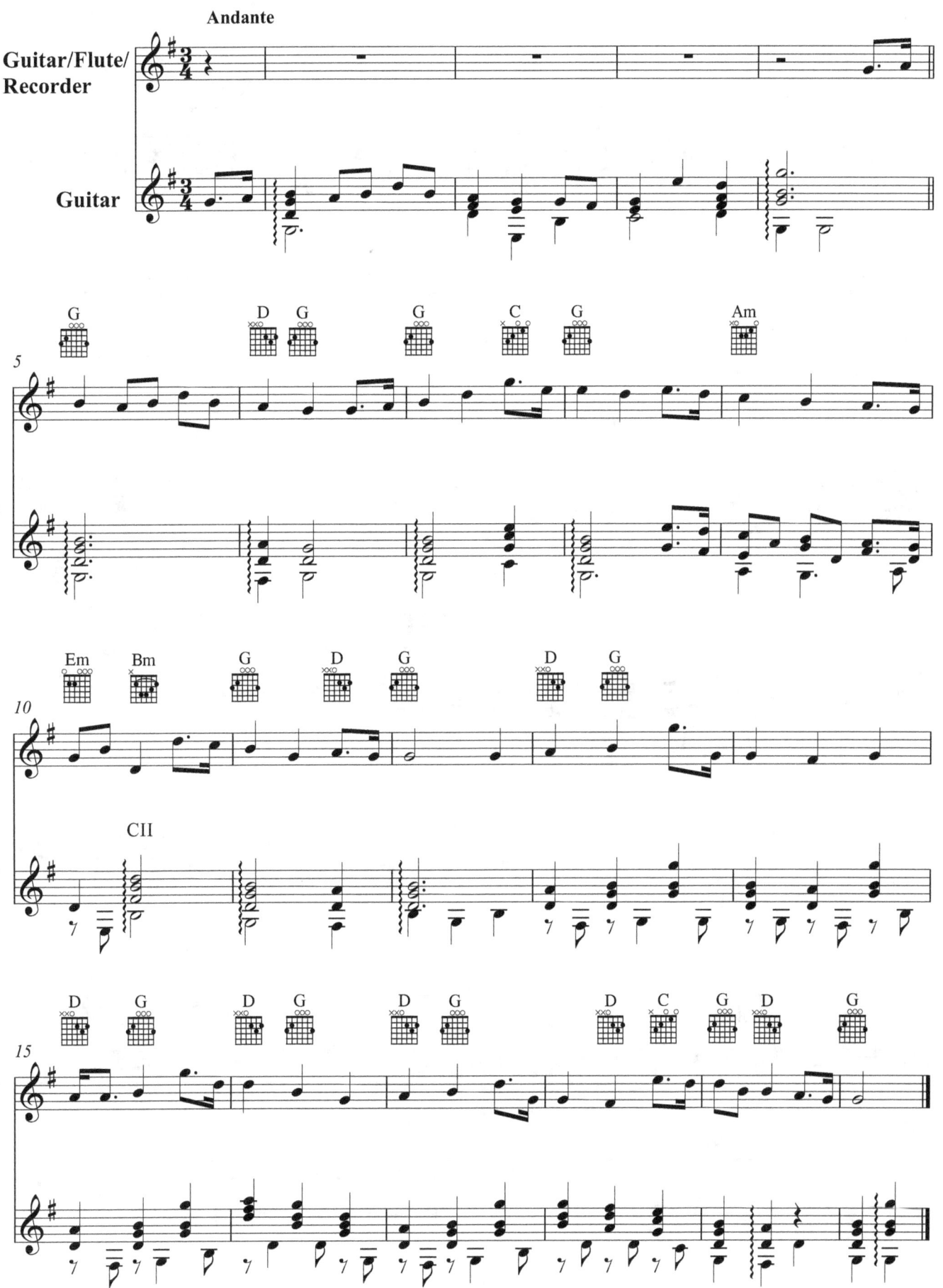

Mary Morison

Robert Burns

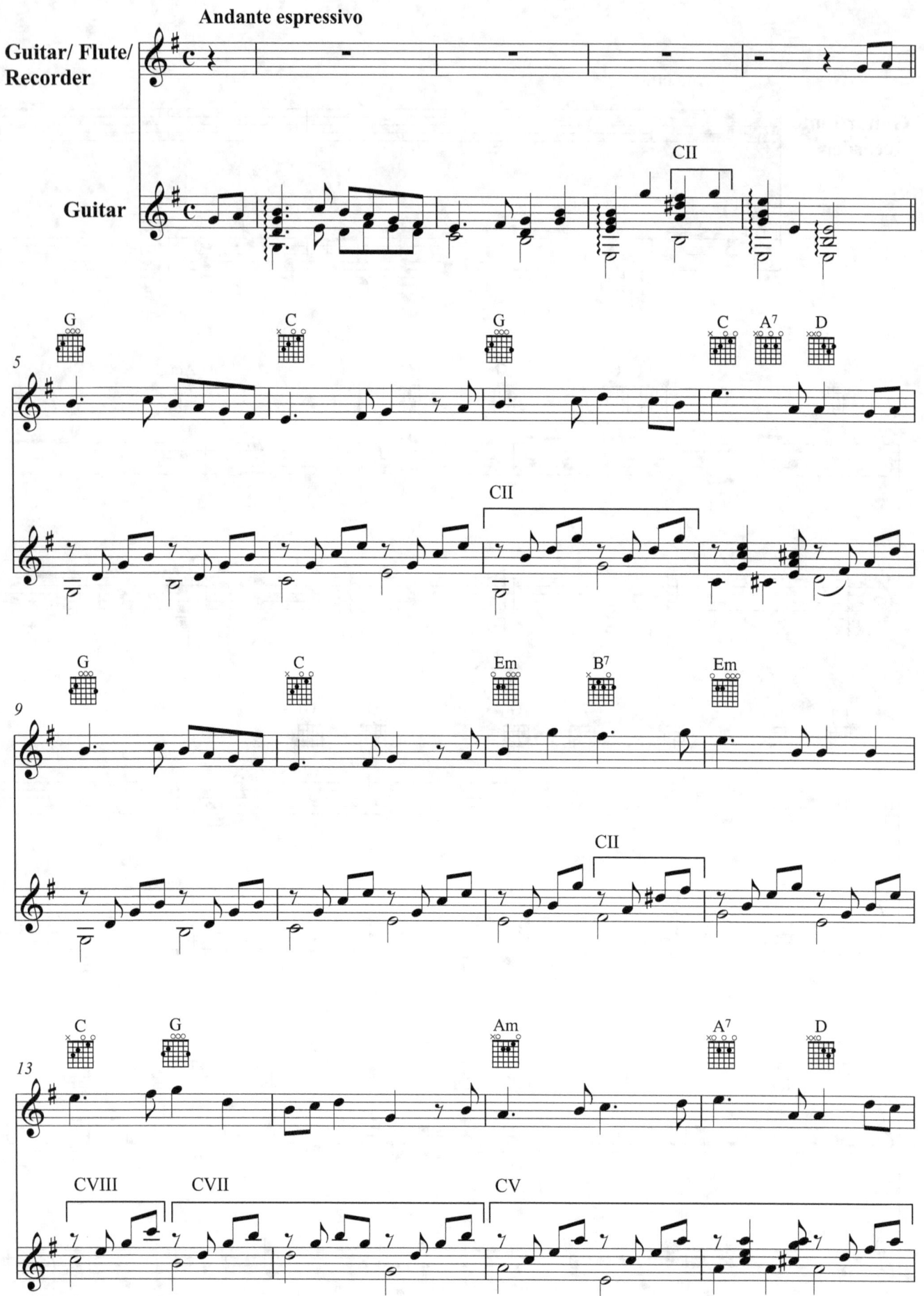

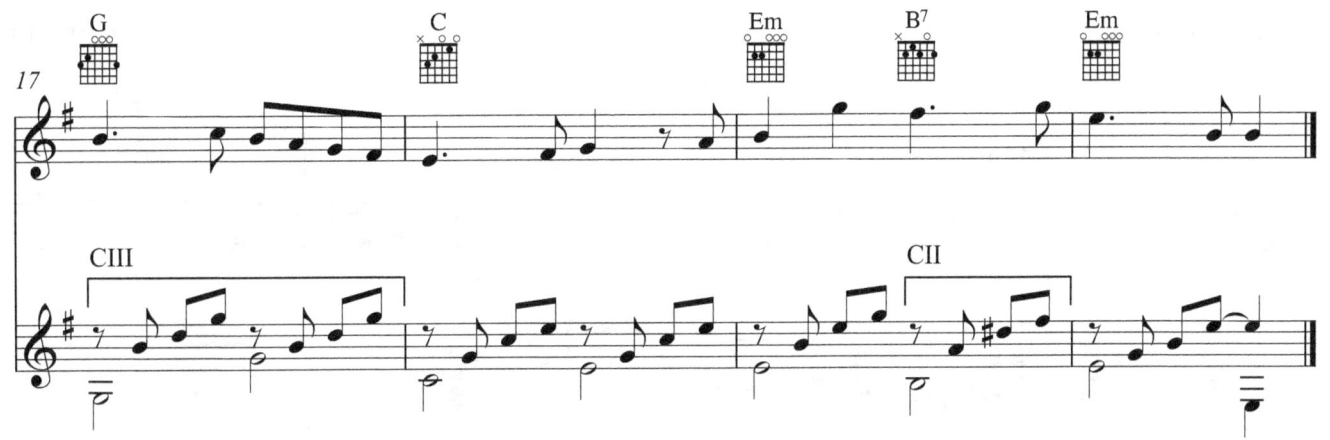

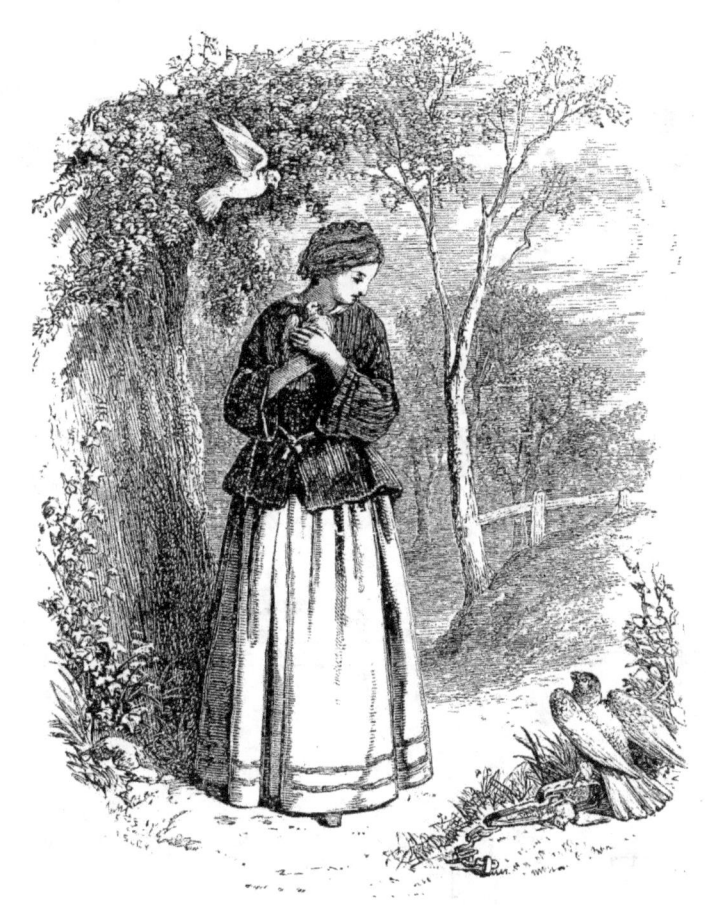

My Nannie's Awa'!

Robert Burns

Traditional

Appendix 2: Glossary of Scottish Dialect Used in the Songs

A' – all

Ae - one

Aft - oft

Aften – often

Alane - alone

Amang – among

An – and

Ance – once

Anither - another

Auld - old

Awa – away

Bear – barley

Bide – abide, endure

Blawn - blown

Blink – glance

Braid - broad

Brak - broke

Bonie/ bonnie – beautiful

Canna – cannot

Cantie – cheerful

Dine – Dinner time

Drap – drop

Drouk – to wet

E'er – ever

Fain - fond

Fuase – false

Fit – foot

Frae – from

Gaed – went

Gie – give

Gowans - daisies

Gowd – gold

Gude - good

Hae – have

Hame - home

Hoddin – the motion of a countryman riding a cart-horse

Ingle – fireplace

Jo - dear

Lang – long

Loe'd – loved

Loof - palm

Mak – make

Mailin – a farm

Mavis – a thrush

Meikle - much

Mirk – dark

Maun - must

Muanna – musn't

Nae- not

Naething – nothing

O' – of

Owre – over

Paidl'd - paddled

Pint Stowp – pint cup

Poud - picked

Pu'ing - picking

Puir – poor

Pund - pound

Sae – so

Sin – since

Sma' – small

Snaw - snow

Sodger – soldier

Stane – stone

Stourie - dusty

Tentless – careless

Thegither - together

Till – to

Tither – the other

Trysted – appointed

Trysting - meeting

Twa – two

Waught - draught

Wha – who

Whase - whose

Wi – with

Wille – will

Ye'll – You'll

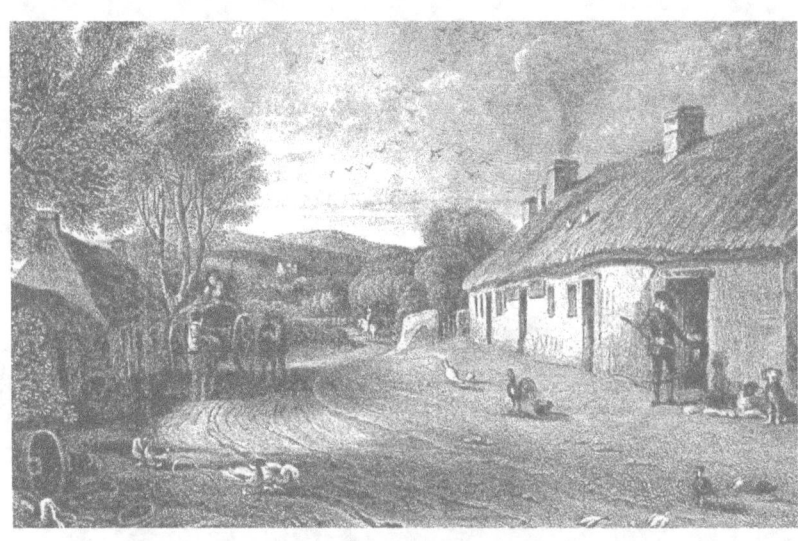

The cottage in Alloway where Burns was born

Ukulele Chord Diagrams for Songs in this Book

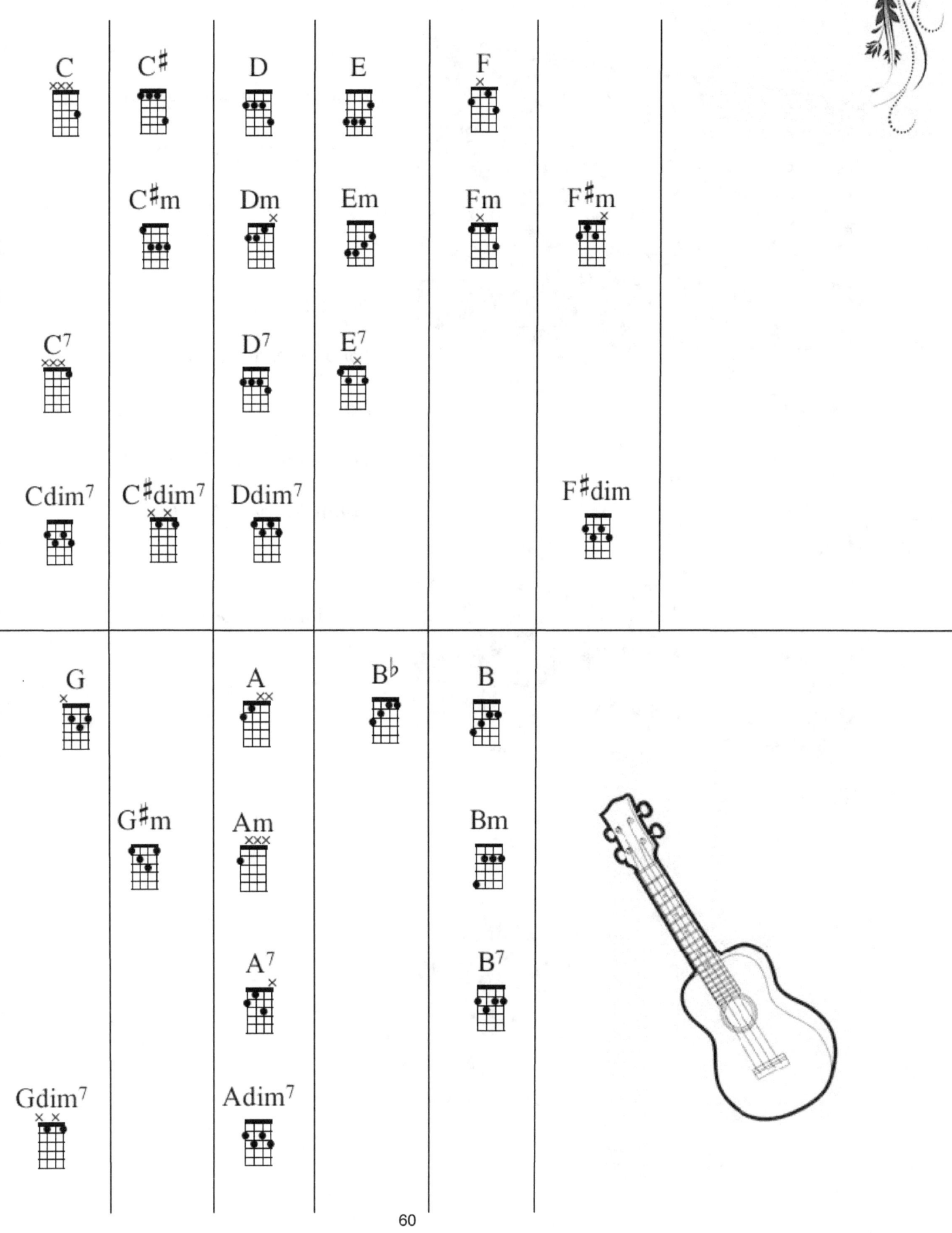

By the same author:

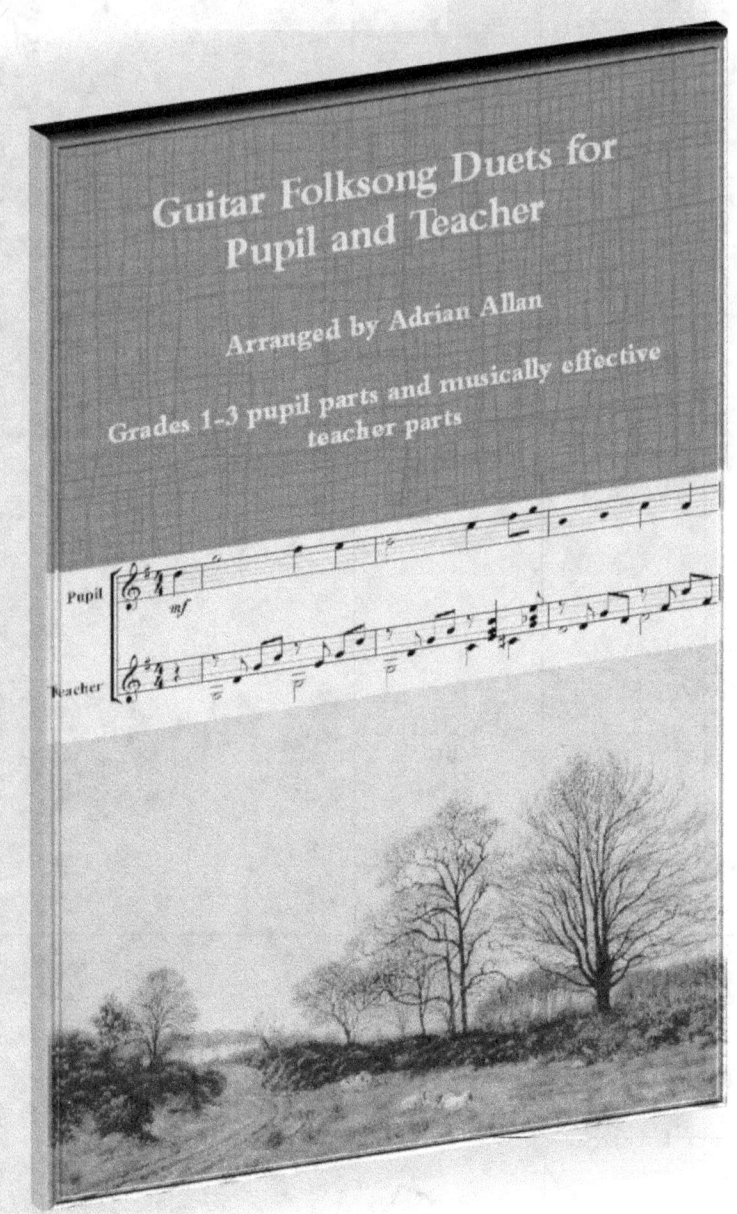

A selection of early-grade popular

folksongs supported by

Interesting teacher parts, including:

Annie Laurie

Londonderry Air/ Danny Boy

Down by the Sally Gardens

The Lincolnshire Poacher

Bonny Mary of Argyle

...and many more

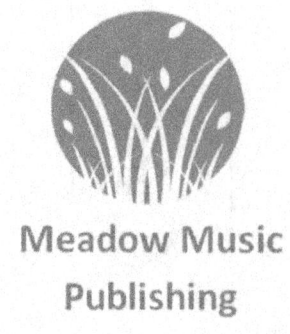

Meadow Music
Publishing

www.ingramcontent.com/pod-product-compliance
Lightning Source LLC
Chambersburg PA
CBHW081049170526
45158CB00006B/1911